WILD THYMES

CATERING to the EGOS of the Hollywood *Elite*

Sally Van Slyke

Camino
Diablo
Press

Camino Diablo Press

WILD THYMES / Catering to the EGOS of the Hollywood Elite
www.wildthymesbook.com

Published in the United States of America
All right reserved.
© 2012 Camino Diablo Press

Library of Congress Control Number /LCCN: 2011945893

Storage Area Network / SAN: 860-3367
Autobiography / Memoir

ISBN: 978-0-9852820-0-4

First Edition, 2012

Cover design, editing and production by:
Klein Graphics / www.kleingraphics.net

Typeface: Warnock Pro - 11 point.

This book is dedicated to my partner,
Gene Kevin Filson
The funniest man with the fewest words anyone ever met.

He was...
"Here Today - Gone To Lunch"

WILD THYMES
Catering to the EGOS of the *Hollywood Elite*

TABLE OF CONTENTS

ACKNOWLEDGEMENTS

Thank you Hollywood for the fun first chapter of my life.

Thank you to all my friends and clients who have so encouraged me over the years to write these stories down and to my kitty and doggies who patiently sat with me until I got it done.

A special thank you to Mick Jagger. Why? Because I can.

I send a twenty-one gun salute to my all-around guru Randy Klein and his alter-ego Larry, who hand-held me through this entire process and, most importantly, edited my stream of consciousness somehow making sense of it all. And, of course, to the great team at Klein Graphics who has proven patience is indeed a virtue.

Great affection and a mentor's pride must go to my Executive Chef Roman Martinez, a super star with knives, and his sidekick Julio Saca who I fire every day but who has kept coming back for fifteen years. To all my Wild Thyme team; I could not have made it through the year without your compassion, support and help.

Love and deep appreciation to my sister Suzie, who is definitely the ying to my yang and to her son, my Emmy-winning nephew Lou, who has far more talent than he gives himself credit for. To my parents for just about everything and Grandma Lilly for being such an exquisite example of a grand lady.

Finally, to Dadee Gene the Bean and his true love Charlotte the Harlot the Only Only Starlit and her brothers Spike Lee, Too and Ho-Hum.

Fly with the Angels 'til I get there.

AUTHOR'S NOTE

Hollywood. I was imperfect in a seemingly perfect world.
I began as a page and rose through the ranks to become an
influential studio insider. Then, at the top of my game
I walked away from it all.

In the following collection of stories, I invite you to come with me as I take you on a behind-the-scenes romp through the sometimes not-so-flattering inner workings of Tinsel Town. During my years as a studio "suit," I was fortunate to collaborate with many of the great filmmakers and stars of this generation. We went eye-to-eye, toe-to-toe, and some-times fist-to-fist. Humorous, poignant, infuriating and often even shock-ing, all the stories have one thing in common—they are absolutely true. I know because I was there, and the tabloids weren't.

These days, when my students, clients, or friends learn of my back-ground, inevitably they want to hear the inside scoop. They ask, "Tell us the truth. What's Robert Redford really like?"

I reply, "Other than that he hates my guts?" With that, we're off to the races.

"You-need-to-write-a-book" is the mantra I have heard over and over again. "I will someday," has been my answer.

A procrastinator at heart, I doubted that someday would ever come.

Now it isn't like I don't have good excuses. I'm not lazy. On the contrary, I currently own a full-service catering and event management company quite by marketing happenstance called *Wild Thyme*, and last year we catered over 130 weddings alone. Although I have a great team backing me up and we all love it, it's still a great deal of work.

So like my beloved Scarlet O'Hara I adopted the attitude, "I'll think about it tomorrow."

Tomorrow came when Gene, my partner of seventeen years, was diagnosed with what turned out to be terminal cancer. He died on May 9, 2011. During the last conversation we were ever to have on this earth, he asked me to promise him just one thing.

Mustering all his strength he whispered, "I want you to write the book."

"I will," I said and crossed my heart.

This book is my promise to him and his last great gift to me.

Gene never cared about Hollywood and all the glitz and glam stuff. But he was always genuinely amused when I'd launch into one of my stories and enjoyed hearing my audience react.

"Sure," I'd say to those listening, "go ahead.... laugh at my pain."

And that's what I'm hoping readers will do; read these stories and laugh at the grand messes I got myself—and often everyone else—into.

Hollywood is all about the illusion of perfection. I was imperfect, because I had suffered from polio as a young girl. As a result, I have two different size feet and a slight limp. I knew heading in that the odds were against me in an unforgiving industry, but I was determined nothing was going to stop me.

I would be the American Dream come true.

I am a lucky person and very blessed. I have enjoyed two successful careers, each in industries where the odds of success are stacked against you.

In the good times and even more in the tough times, I have always known there is an Angel on my shoulder looking out for me. She is also a redhead, but that's another book.

Any time you think of a question for me you can find me on Google, Facebook, Twitter or my websites. I'd love to hear from you.

Until then, see you backstage catering to the famous and infamous!

- Sally Van Slyke

Chapter One

PLAY BALL

Being a part of the Hollywood scene was a life-long dream.
My publicist job was only the first stepping stone to what I hoped
would be greater opportunities. I was not going to wait around,
but I was determined to work hard and make my own luck.

Just five minutes after I was hired as a Metromedia Television staff publicist, I began haranguing the news director for a news reporting assignment. Unfortunately, the answer was always a resounding "No!" Undaunted, I spent many hours hanging around the newsroom desperate to secure that first big break. I'm sure they thought I would eventually give up and go away.

Never. They didn't know me. I knew that persistence would win the game, eventually.

I figured out how to circumvent the news director by becoming tight with the news team and a young talented reporter, Bill Smith. Bill soon became my mentor and friend. Rumors flew. They were true and we did indeed, have a lot of fun together.

Bill was patient and generous with his time. He taught me the ins and outs of interviewing, scripting pithy copy and extracting the maximum umph from the editing process. The first pointer he offered was to start a piece with an arresting sound cue. It startles the viewers and helps them focus on what's happening. Years later the famous horror film director, Wes Craven, gave me the same advice.

After working all day at my publicist desk on the third floor, I raced down to the loading dock to jump aboard the news van with Bill and the crew as they headed out on assignment. These were not the pristine satellite vans they have today, but well-used, dirty, old, white Econovans. Straddling the camera boxes, I strapped myself in with bungee cords.

It was difficult keeping my balance as we careened around corners, rushing to a news story. This kind of ride-along was absolutely verboten. But none of us ever mentioned my being on board to anyone, so fortunately we never were caught.

On scene, Bill conducted his interviews and I observed. When he had what he needed for the story, he handed me the microphone and I stepped in. He watched as I conducted a practice interview of my own. When Bill did a "field wrap" (a story summation) and threw it back to the anchor desk, I did one too.

Back at the studio I stood over Bill's shoulder, while he ran the footage called b-roll. He wrote his report to coincide and intercut with the footage at hand. This was not as easy as it looked. I worked at the console next to him, piecing together just one story while he polished off three.

When I managed to get a story in the can that we all agreed was good, I showed it to the news director. His droll response was, "Nice first try. You need to head to a smaller market like Podunk and earn some credentials. Then we can have a serious talk."

This felt dismissive; but as a general rule a novice reporter didn't work in a major market without having spent the requisite years covering smaller locales. This was standard practice to sharpen a rookie's edge. Los Angeles is the second largest television market in the United States, falling between New York at number one and Chicago in third. Nobody starts in LA!

Oh yeah? Well, I would prove them wrong even if it killed me. Just showing up was not enough, so I needed to take another approach. I wasn't getting anywhere with the news director, so I began to hound the program director as well. He had the power to put me on air, too.

I looked for an opportunity and found it in the Pasadena Rose Parade. Every New Year's Day, Metromedia Channel 11 covered the annual event. It was a huge undertaking and involved a large commentary team.

I approached the program director. "Why can't I be part of the commentary team along the parade route?" I asked him.

At first the answer was a deafening, "No!"

As it happened, my publicist desk was next door to the program director's office. I happened to overhear him take a call from the color commentator who was scheduled to fill the 4 pm to midnight slot. He had fallen ill. I peeked my head into his office. He knew I was the only viable option available on such short notice. I got the nod!

Miss Green Sleeves Sally, with her field crew, was going out to get live shots of the streets of Pasadena. No script to work from and no one holding my hand. This was the big time. My crew and I headed out in a brand new satellite van. It was the van's first trial run too. The crew was overwhelmed just figuring out how the satellite worked and had no time for any of my questions. The enormity of what I was attempting to do sunk in. This was more complicated than I expected. I was to host a five-minute live cut-in at the top of each hour.

I was in charge. So it was up to me to select the location based on what I thought viewers would find interesting. When I say no script, I mean no script. I could talk to anyone, including the average Joe on the street, the float decorators, the flower shippers, the animal wranglers, or even the animals for that matter.

"Just make it visual," they said. My job was to entice viewers to tune into Channel 11 the next morning instead of our competition. We had to promise the brightest, most comprehensive coverage of the parade. That was the main message I was to get across.

The truth is, the floats appear far larger and more beautiful on camera than in person.

During the parade, commentators sit high over Colorado Boulevard in an observation booth and work from a carefully scripted parade "Bible." This huge script includes descriptions such as, "The Veterans Administration gives a nod to Spring with this next breathtaking recreation of Victoria's famous Buchart Gardens. This eighteen-foot extravaganza is comprised of over three thousand King Alfred daffodils, twenty-five hundred crocuses which were especially cultivated by..." All of these are read verbatim.

Then the second commentator might jump in with what seems like an ad lib, "You know Bob, when I was a little girl my parents took me to see Buchart Gardens, and it was as colorful and romantic as this float is today..."

TV Guide announcement of
Sally on the Morning News Show.

I was always off-script since I did not have one. My crew and I drove around Pasadena searching for something interesting. When we found it, I jumped out and coerced people to talk with me as my crew set up. I interviewed the Montrose High School Majorettes as the band practiced, *California Here I Come,* in the background. I talked to decorators who'd been awake for forty straight hours but were still gung-ho as they pasted the last petals and pumpkin seeds on their float. I stuck my microphone in the snout of petting zoo animals as I grunted along with them. A bevy of potbellied pigs, for instance, were there to ride on the Del Monte farm fresh float in the morning. I tailed judges as they made their various *Best Of...* award decisions, attempting to get the inside skinny. In between cut-ins, we headed to the official Rose Parade House and hoisted a few hot toddies, sans the hooch.

Finally we hit the street again for the last two cut-ins. Colorado Boulevard was now teeming with drunks, street hawkers, musicians, and tourists from all over the country. Most had created makeshift campsites along the parade route to secure a good viewing location. I interviewed Siamese twins dressed as a pot of petunia's (which I must say was a great visual) and a gentleman riding a giant unicycle who, caught on tape, looked like he was trying to run me over. I conducted an interview with him by stretching the microphone way over my head to pick up his answers.

At the stroke of midnight, from a precarious perch on the back of a 50's Chevy convertible, I wished greater Los Angeles a "Happy New Year." My final cut-in showed me rolling down the boulevard surrounded by dozens of inebriated young men all acting like USC frat boys.

It was a long day, but I truly had the time of my life. More importantly, the station was happy with my work and the cut-ins were deemed a huge success. I received a very gracious note from the program director with a check for a whopping $1,000, which was unexpected and a big deal to me at the time.

I'd worn those guys down and was well on my way. The following year I was selected to host the hour-long Annual Children's Holiday Faire. This festive party resembled a traditional carnival with rides, video games, hotdogs, cotton candy...the works. Channel 11 invited their employee's kids, along with children from under-privileged homes and local orphanages. As they left, each child received a hand-wrapped present appropriate for their gender and age to take home and place under the tree. The hour of edited highlights was broadcast on Christmas Day. So we were lucky if even three viewers actually watched it. So what? I was out there learning my stuff and in Los Angeles no less.

Metromedia Channel 11 was the official Dodger baseball station. Veteran sportscaster, Vin Scully, covered the televised games. An accomplished sports junky by the name of Bob Hiestand directed the game coverage, including pre-game and post-game segments. Each was fifteen minutes in length.

I grew up loving baseball. My father had only daughters and always treated my sister and me to the Giant's games when they played the Atlanta Braves (previously the Boston Braves). My father grew up in Boston and remained loyal to this franchise until the end.

I approached Bob Hiestand requesting a favor. "May I be allowed to host a pre-game or post-game show?"

He said, "Yes, if you can come up with an interesting angle and get one of the players to agree to talk with you on camera."

Inspired and armed with a press badge, I hung out next to the Dodger dugout with my camera. Pretending to photograph the game, I was actually just getting to know some of the players. Considering several angles, I settled on a pre-game interview with the starting pitcher. Generally starting pitchers don't want to have anything to do with the cameras before a game. However, I suspected veteran Don Sutton might, because he wanted to become a broadcaster when his pitching days were over. So why not help me out, and get some on-air practice in? I ran this idea past Bob.

Don Sutton was a fun guy who sported a blond curly fro and impish grin to go with his Dodger blue. Bracing myself for rejection, I approached him in front of the other players before the game. If he said yes, I was on. If he said no, Bob would take the pre-game show in another direction with stock footage.

Sutton agreed amidst loud guffaws from his teammates. After warm-ups, I sidled over to him and we began. Every educated and profound pitching question I asked was met with a funny answer. He wasn't taking me seriously at all. At one point he asked me if I liked his new perm. I told him I didn't realize he permed his hair.

"Oh yeah, helps with the pitching," he said as he grabbed my hand and put it on his head. "You're really cute," he added.

Someone in the outfield threw a ground ball in our direction and, looking up, I realized a whole group of jocks were laughing up a storm. Bob Hiestand was getting the biggest kick of all.

"Real cute fellas," I barked. "You're tanking my career."

It seems that Al Kriven, one of the senior Metromedia executives in charge of all five Metromedia stations across the country, happened to catch the pre-game show that evening. He loved me on camera. What seemed like a big practical joke at the time turned out to be the boost I was looking for.

Sally interviewing Don Sutton

Sally at Dodger Field covering pre-game.

LOS ANGELES TIMES WEEKLY LISTINGS AUGUST 2 • AUGUST 8, 1981

TELEVISION TIMES

Robert Vaughn portrays ambitious newspaper publisher who sensationalizes the news and Susan Sullivan is his wife on "City of Fear" Sunday night in an ABC movie at 9 p.m.

ON THE COVER — Prince Charles and Lady Diana Spencer's royal wedding will be telecast live beginning at 2 a.m. Wednesday on ABC and NBC. CBS begins at 4 a.m. Covering the affair will be ABC's Barbara Walters and Peter Jennings, CBS' David Frost and Dan Rather, and NBC's Tom Brokaw.

Rodney Dangerfield guests as an elevator operator with the star of "The Robert Klein Show," a new comedy special on NBC Friday at 9 p.m.

KTTV's Sally Van Slyke reports on plastic and reconstructive surgery in a five-part investigative series on fastest growing medical specialty beginning Monday, Channel 11 at 10:30 p.m.

Television Times article announcing feature on cosmetic surgery.

Then and there the news director decided to give me the chance to do a little field reporting. I put together feature reports and anchored them myself on the evening's ten o'clock broadcast. One such five-part series reported on plastic and reconstructive surgery. I took the cameras inside the operating room and showed the procedures from nose jobs to breast implants. I stood beside the doctor and watched as he operated. When the surgeon demonstrated his basic hemstitch sutures by sliding the thread back and forth through the eyelid, I knew we had some footage that would entice viewers. This was squeamishly eye-catching stuff.

We photographed a man named Rudy, who upon arriving at Cedars-Sinai emergency room, required immediate plastic surgery to put his face back together. The surgeon I was working with on the series called me at home to immediately, "come take a look."

Donning scrubs, I inched my way forward in the operating room and was aghast at what I saw, or to put it more succinctly, what I couldn't see. I literally could not distinguish the top of this man's face from the bottom. Interviewing the cops and medic's who brought him in, I learned he'd been riding a bicycle when a huge semi truck hit him full on. The surgeon, after five hours of piecing this face together as best he could, explained that if it wasn't for Rudy's mustache he would have had far greater difficulty determining what went where.

I interviewed the reconstructed Rudy for the series after he had gone through ten operations. Ten down and one to go to replace part of a missing tip of his nose. The result was simply amazing. He had a few very visible scars, but perfectly shaped features, and a winning smile.

During this series, I met a wonderful woman named Goldie. A victim of breast cancer, she'd lost her left breast two years before and was thinking of having a reconstruction. Her husband wasn't in favor of the surgery. He loved her the way she was. She was straddling the fence. So I asked her to show me her scar so I could give her my opinion. Off came her blouse. The scar was certainly not off putting or ugly. A simple X marked the spot.

I voted for whichever way she wanted to go. We talked for over an hour that afternoon and mutually agreed it was about time women stopped being so terribly frightened about the reported mutilation they would suffer if they needed this kind of surgery.

Goldie decided she'd like to do something positive for women in her situation. She spontaneously volunteered to take off her blouse and show the world her mastectomy scar if we didn't reveal her face. It was a brave thing to do. Our cameras zoomed in for a close-up look. One breast was gone, the other remained, and there was nothing horrifying about it. Goldie later opted for no surgery.

Each night of the week-long series I was allowed to *hype* my segment by showing snippets of key footage during the news updates every half hour. I would say something like "Join me at ten when I'll have the fourth in my five-part series on plastic and reconstructive surgery. We'll show you what a mastectomy scar looks like and talk to a brave woman debating reconstruction."

Ratings for that week jumped two whole points every night. I am most proud that, to my knowledge, I was the first on-air news journalist to show viewers an actual mastectomy scar.

Still functioning as the staff publicist during the day, I was forced to hijack crews and tape these segments in the early morning or late at night. Getting a kick out of my guts and gall, the crews were great in helping me by going way above and beyond the call of duty. Bill Smith lobbied for me to become a featured part of the morning news broadcast that he anchored. Often he'd get his way. Then I'd take my lunch from eleven to twelve, run to the bathroom, fix my own makeup, jump on set, read my piece and head back to my publicist desk.

My staff publicist position paid $18,000 a year. Each time I appeared on the news I was paid the AFTRA (The American Federation of Television and Radio Artists) minimum of fifty-two dollars a segment. When my piece ran on other Metromedia stations across the country I did not receive additional compensation.

I was broke.

I found another job on Saturdays working the reception desk at a well-known skin care specialists shop in Beverly Hills at the rate of $100 a day. The owner was a Belgium woman by the name of Aida Grey. She was a tiny terror but a redhead like me, so we got along famously. She became my go-to expert for special segments I put together on skin care and

Sally with Bill Smith

nutrition. Her face scrub was made of almonds and honey and was amazing. This woman was way ahead of the times.

One of my favorite special reports with Miss Grey told of the time a baby had gotten hold of its mother's face scrub and proceeded to eat the whole jar. The infant was rushed to the hospital by hysterical parents, who were smart enough to take along the empty container. The emergency room doctor tested the product and announced that there was no problem. In fact, their baby would benefit from this fully nutritious meal. All the while baby was happily gurgling.

One evening towards the end of my Metromedia years, I was asked to rush up to Dodger Stadium to host the post-game show. This was new to me. I'd only hosted a few pre-game segments up to this point primarily because the post-game shows often took the cameras inside the locker room where women were not welcome.

The Dodgers won the game that evening and quickly headed into the exclusivity of the locker room. I stood outside the door as they pushed right past me. Jocks can be jerks. No one glanced in my direction let alone stopped, though they could see I was desperate for a post-game interview.

I was furious. "Okay guys, let's play hard ball." I sent word ahead I was going into the locker room.

When I got there, twenty or so Dodgers dropped their towels in unison to the floor exposing themselves. They all stared straight at me smiling. I turned bright red, and felt myself start to shake so badly my knees were knocking. You might remember some players on this team including Dusty Baker, Ron Cey, and Steve Garvey. Of course, they expected me to turn tail and run, but I held my ground.

My now totally jacked cameraman, the lunatic named Rex shouted at me, "Tell me what you want to shoot!"

"Tight head shots," I snapped back.

I proceeded to interview two or three of the players closest to me, which wasn't that close. When these guys suddenly twigged to the fact that I wasn't going to run in terror, but was seriously going to do my job, some had the smarts to duck behind locker doors. The others should consider themselves lucky that YouTube didn't yet exist.

Needless to say, my cavalier action that night caused quite a stir. Many pundits didn't agree with my decision and let me know it. My news story was a news story in its own right. If I offended some, then tough!

Years later, I still feel a sense of accomplishment and pride when I see women commentators freely accessing locker rooms everywhere. Let's give a hand to women's lib.

Play ball, girls.

13

Chapter Two

BETTE DAVIS EYES

Parties are an oxymoron in Hollywood.

The word party brings to mind people gathering in the spirit of friendship prepared to have a good time. Hollywood "parties" are never about having a good time. They are strictly business.

The spirit of friendship, embraced by those folks who fill the theatre seats, never rears its ugly head at a Hollywood party. Rather, these star-studded soirées are simply industry events affording attendees the opportunity to smile and kiss-kiss with all those people one usually tries to out think, out produce, out smart, out sell, or just plain sell out.

Movie premieres that are photographed so beautifully for news-magazine and television shows can be especially dismal. A studio spends hundreds of thousands of dollars on lavish movie premieres to entertain their competitors' executives knowing these suits will be compelled to hate everything about the entire evening. Especially when the picture is really good.

"All for one and one for all." What idiot wrote that?

Of course, not every event is a premiere or awards ceremony. There are also those altruistic, star-studded charity events you've read so much about. These soirées are fueled by Hollywood's ongoing penchant for giving where power-players wrangle for cachet and cash. Players and struggling wannabes have to make an appearance during the evening unless they can come up with a good no-show excuse like being in rehab locked-down.

Just two weeks after I arrived on the national entertainment publicity scene at Rogers & Cowan Public Relations, I was assigned to coordinate a huge event honoring Aaron Spelling. At the time, Aaron was the hottest television producer in town. His shows included Dynasty, Hart to Hart, The Love Boat, Fantasy Island, Charlie's Angels, and more. Spelling was our largest television account. So when you think about it, he paid most of my new salary.

The charity benefiting from the event contributed absolutely nothing to the evening except to provide a small guest list and throw together a dinner committee who only got in the way. In truth, it was the public relations minions who did all the work.

I was such a minion.

Aaron passed the word down via his other more established minions that he wanted me to find a hot singer for the evening's requisite entertainment. And, by the way, Mr. or Ms. "Really Hot" had to donate their services, which meant paying their own union musicians, lighting, and stagehand crew. This was a very costly request. There ain't nothin' free in Hollywood. Ever.

But it was clear I was to die trying to find the perfect person. Someone who wanted something in return perhaps? I called agents, managers...ex- lovers. You name him or her and I called them.

They all laughed.

Then serendipity struck. Late one night, I tuned in to the TV just in time to catch the legendary sex symbol Tom Jones on the Tonight Show. He was mumbling to Johnny, "Ya know, I'd like to do some acting."

Hell yes I knew now. And here I came—*Delilah racing over the green, green grass of home.*

Hollywood emulates our nation's capitol. To succeed, you must learn to master the art of misinformation. With this in mind, I tracked down Tom's manager. I told him Aaron had always loved Tom's singing, admired his creative genius, and was thrilled to learn that he wanted to try his hand at acting.

Now for the big finish.

If Tom would agree to donate a performance to Aaron's upcoming "honoration" there could be a guest-starring role with his name on it in an upcoming episode of *The Love Boat*. His manager, a toughie named Gordon, would run it past his client.

Minutes later, Gordon called back to say we had a deal. Of course, there was one tiny missing piece: I had no idea how I was going to make good on this deal. Well...I'd worry about that tomorrow. Today I had a hot act lined up! Hot enough for Aaron anyway. (Personally, I would have preferred Mick.)

Meanwhile, the Dinner Committee was hard at work suggesting things be done *their way*. Aaron's blond wife Candy, currently enjoying the status of first lady of Beverly Hills, demanded we do things *her way*. And so this power play continued with us minions stuck in the middle.

The Committee designed a very understated, ivory-paper card invitation. In stark contrast, Candy designed a very colorful invitation. She demanded it be placed in a gift box, ornately wrapped and hand delivered to each potential guest by her own Beverly Hills shop personnel.

The Committee designated modest cocktail attire. Candy dictated black tie.

The Committee shunned using a dais. Candy insisted on a giant dais. Further, she saw no reason to seat any charity representatives on this elevated platform. She instructed me to see to it that she was seated on her husband's right.

Then with only a week left to go, Aaron called me personally. He had just cast the two-time Oscar winner Bette Davis in his new TV series *Hotel*. Miss Davis was his latest and greatest coup, and he wanted the honor of her presence at his dinner. He commanded me to get her there. No excuses.

I'm sure it seems obvious to the uninitiated. The easy way to do this was for Aaron to call Miss Davis and invite her personally. If he had, however, it would be construed as asking for a favor. Favors are a high-priced commodity in Hollywood. You ask, you owe. Aaron did not want to owe Miss Davis anything.

Bette Davis was fully aware of this little industry minuet, and had no intention of being a pushover. We exchanged at least a dozen phone calls before she agreed to attend. And to make things interesting, she would only show up if she was seated on Aaron's right. Oh geez—someone give me a break!

Finally, while I was still breathing, the evening arrived. As predicted, everyone who was anyone showed up. I stood at the door, a receiving line of one, officially greeting every elegantly sequined, bejeweled guest.

In Hollywood it is all about the entrance.

The night of the charity event, strobes blazed as Candy swept out of a white Rolls Royce limo holding little daughter Tori's hand. She was wearing a full-length Venetian lace gown and sporting a necklace that *Women's Wear Daily* would describe as, "a monumental ocean of sparkling diamonds and emeralds."

But for all the preliminary glitter it was Miss Davis who made the most dramatic entrance. She arrived last escorted by film historian Robert Osborne. Last is always best. The famous siren posed theatrically for the photographers, tossing red roses to the crowd of onlookers. In her best Jezebel, smoke-filled voice, she repeated the sentiment, "Farewell. Farewell. You'll all miss me when I'm gone."

Now if Miss Davis was suffering from a sense of mortality this night she certainly didn't show it. Seated on Aaron's right (let's face it, I was more scared of Bette than of Candy) the old gal was in top Hollywood form. She kicked back more than a few vodkas and basked in her iconic status.

But when Tom Jones hit the stage our little, five-foot grandma became completely unhinged. To everyone's utter amazement, she leaped like a young gazelle onto the dais table and boogied her booty all through his act. *Even the ballads!* Tom is used to the Vegas scene, but even so, this poor guy began to sweat more than usual.

It took at least ten minutes for the room to quiet down after the spectacle was over. Then, as the speeches began, I felt a tap on my shoulder. Someone whispered in my ear, "Miss Davis wants to see you."

"Now?" I asked.

"Oh yeah! Right now." This was said in such a way that I knew not to argue.

I wondered just how the hell I was going to accomplish this. She was propped up just one seat away from the speaker. I couldn't simply saunter up behind the guy to have a brief tête-à-tête with Bette. On the other hand, there was no telling what the vixen would do if I didn't get to her and fast. So, I hoisted up my new figure-hugging, fully-beaded gown and crawled in the dark on all-fours onto the raised dais floor. Finally I managed to come face-to-thigh with the legendary movie icon.

"There you are at last. What took you so long?" The famous staccato resounded through the room.

"Shhhhhh!" I whispered.

"Don't tell me to shush...I want.....Tom Jones....NOW. Go...find him.... bring him here. *This instant!*"

"Okay, Miss Davis. Absolutely. Right away." I wiggled backwards, trying not to draw too much attention.

I found Tom enjoying a drink he paid for himself ensconced in a suite for which he was also picking up the tab. I delivered the message. He

After changing her outfit, Sally relaxes with Tom Jones as they share a drink together.

turned white as a ghost. "Pleeeese...didn't you see her? Do I hafta go?"

"Yes. Without question. Believe me, it can still get a lot worse," I assured him.

Hand-in-hand, we made our way up to the front. Mr. Studdly was literally clinging to me for dear life. There was Miss Davis perched on the corner of the dais, legs crossed and puff-puffing on her trademark cigarette. Luckily, the speeches were over.

If I live to be a thousand I am positive I will never witness another "act" like the one this legend performed for the benefit of the Welsh crooner that night. Before my eyes, eighty years evaporated from her face as she transformed into the young flirtatious starlet she once was. Mr. Jones played his role well, too. He was at once charming, flustered, sweet and appropriately embarrassed. The ol' gal loved it.

Watching Tom, it occurred to me that he might actually be great in a role on *The Love Boat.* But I had no time to dwell on such magical thoughts. Out of the corner of my eye I spied Aaron and Tom's manager heading towards me. So I did exactly what all good movie flimflam artists do. I got the hell out of there fast. Poof!

As it turned out, Tom Jones never got the opportunity to appear on *The Love Boat,* but it was not my fault. Soon after that evening, ABC canceled the show and Captain Stubing and his crew sailed into the celluloid sunset for the last time.

Just weeks later, Miss Davis, following a diagnosis of breast cancer, was forced to drop out of the cast of *Hotel.* Had she known about her condition that night? Is that what she had meant by "you'll miss me when I'm gone?" Who knows? Either way, she certainly had one hell of a last hurrah!

Chapter Three

DYNASTY BULLION

Sometimes when the Hollywood glitter hits the fan,
you have to spin it into gold.

I think back to the time when the two nighttime soap operas, *Dallas* and *Dynasty,* competed with each other for the top Nielsen rating each week. If you're too young to ponder that far back—imagine *Dancing With The Stars* against *American Idol.* At the end of each season, the soaps really went at it, cliffhanger to cliffhanger. It was never really a contest though; *Dallas* always won! Who will ever forget, "Who Shot J.R.?" Certainly not their advertisers!

One year, Alexis Carrington, the shrew we all loved to hate, was trapped by raging fire in a high-rise building that looked like it was about to become a pile of smoldering ash. The season ended with a freeze frame of Alexis, totally seething. Millions worldwide were left to ponder the fate of this beloved vixen. Would the old bitch escape, or perhaps emerge fried over easy and in need of plastic surgery? Viewers had no choice but to live in suspense until September...or at least until the tabloids reported Joan Collins had inked her new contract.

For each season, we—the flacksters in charge of *Dynasty's* image—were given a budget of twenty thousand dollars to come up with a September season opening stunt. What, pray tell, could we do this time to light the scorch torch for yet another season of irresistible drivel?

I got it! We'd lease prime electronic billboard space in key cities. Timed to run every sixty seconds, these billboards would flash "Burn, Alexis, Burn!" in neon lights and then erupt into a ball of flames shooting into the sky. We decided to premiere our stunt at a Hollywood location. Joan could be on hand to ignite the flames herself.

My team loved this idea. The producers loved this idea. More importantly, ABC climbed onboard and agreed to pony up the extra few hundred "K" this would cost.

Fabulous. "Burn, Alexis, Burn!" would sizzle off lips across this hemisphere.

But when Joan Collins got wind of our plan, she went ballistic.

At midnight my phone rang. On the other end was "Alexis" herself.

"Have you all lost your bloody minds?? I don't need some lunatic torching my house, because he saw it on some fucking billboard. This is not going to happen."

"But, Joan...," I stammered.

Slam. The line went dead.

Naturally, when called on the carpet by agents and lawyers, the producers of *Dynasty* swore up and down to Joan that they *never* considered the billboard idea as viable.

"What are those idiot publicists thinking?" the producers and studio execs exclaimed in tandem.

Then everyone looked at me.

"Uhmmmm"

I firmly believe that desperation is at the root of many great ideas, and we were certainly desperate. We were being paid to come up with a stunt, and if we wanted to keep getting paid, we had better come up with something incredible—*we had only two weeks!*

We needed a miracle and we got one.

One of my associates, a great lady by the name of Beebe Kline, was in the loop on everything going on in Hollywood. She was a fabulous woman who never forgot a face or a name. Over the course of her long career at Rogers & Cowan she represented many famous stars, including the legendary Sophia Loren, who considered Beebe a best friend.

While I was moaning to Beebe about our *Dynasty* dilemma, she mentioned her plans to attend the upcoming L.A. Fashion Week. This event is held each September and attended by hundreds of fashion editors from around the globe.

A light went on in my brain. I asked her if she thought staging a *Dynasty* fashion extravaganza would be a good idea. Would it be possible to fit it into the already crowded fashion week schedule of *real* fashion shows?

Beebe Kline would have made a skilled diplomat because people just loved working with her. She did her magic and pulled in some big favors for me. The fashion show idea could work.

Dynasty's fashion designer, Nolan Miller, was thrilled with the idea. The producers, however, hated it. Thank goodness Nolan won the day and we had a green light. Well, sort of. In trying to kill the plan, the producers cut our budget to just $5,000! But us publicists are stubborn, tenacious types.

This fashion extravaganza would happen.

Of course, a slim budget meant we could forget about renting the Hilton Ballroom and frankly, Motel Six seemed a bit sketchy.

I managed to coerce the management of a semi-trendy Beverly Hills restaurant adjacent to the fashion show venue into renting us their space for three hours on a Sunday afternoon. This cost us the entire $5,000 but, hey, they agreed to throw in the tea and cookies. More importantly, I could physically make it work. We transformed their long rectangular dining room into a runway. We built an elevated platform at one end where the camera crews and photographers had just enough room to jam together, elbow to ribs, to capture all the glittery action.

With our coffers now empty, hiring *Vogue* cover models was not an option. The only "live mannequins" we could afford were students of a local Hollywood modeling school.

These girls were lacking in sophistication and still on their way to being thin.

Of course, our parade of chiffon and linen was garnered from the stars previous season's outfits and gowns. We had to make these size zeros and ones fit on our runway wannabes. There was simply no time or budget to construct new garments. So Nolan's alteration ladies went on

Sally with Joan Collins

FULL ALERT, pushing and squeezing. The price was right—free. Well folks, ya get whatcha pay for.

"Suck it in, honey." Zip. "Ow!"

My next job was to approach the dashing Blake Carrington, otherwise known as veteran actor John Forsythe, and convince him to be the commentator. John was a lovely man, but didn't see himself as a fashion guru. I convinced him otherwise with my personal guarantee that his script would be tongue-in-cheek, witty, and fun—and it would be, as soon as I got around to writing it.

We didn't have time to send out formal invitations. Remember, there was no email available then. All we could do was notify the fashion editors by circulating flyers, and distributing personal invitations signed by the cast to their hotel rooms literally only one day before the event. A simple photo alert was sent to the national and local news divisions. We had absolutely no idea if anyone would show up, but we rolled the dice.

They came up sixes.

The doors opened to long lines of curious guests waiting to enter. They were packed in like sardines. What a great frantic scene: fashion editors enjoying tea with Hollywood's elite. The forty domestic and international camera crews behaved well for once and took turns stepping onto our makeshift platform. Over a hundred more paparazzi waited outside the doors, all clamoring to get in.

John began, "And this is the beautiful Suzanna wearing a two-piece Chinese red Shantung gown, accented by the Carrington family diamonds. This ensemble was originally worn by my second wife Crystal as she duked it out with my first wife Alexis...."

To be honest, the show *didn't* come off without a hitch. Two pages of John's script stuck together resulting in much hilarity as he described,

Sally with John Forsythe

"...a seductive peignoir my sweet Crystal wore on our second honey-moon...." Meanwhile, our model was traversing the runway wearing an English riding habit complete with a crop.

Our lovely modelettes missed several cues and could be seen peaking at the audience from behind the curtain and giggling, which is a runway no, no.

At last, the famous *Dynasty* theme swelled to a crescendo and divas Joan Collins and Linda Evans glided out onto the catwalk, hand-in-hand, swathed in gold and silver lame evening gowns and glittering with Cartier diamonds. All hell broke loose. Camera crews scrambled and pummeled over each other for the best shot. Editors stood up and cheered. It was sheer, glorious pandemonium.

Talk about snatching victory from the jaws of defeat!

The next day, this finale photograph ran on the front page of hundreds of newspapers. *Entertainment Tonight* dedicated an entire show to us. Executives of several large clothing manufacturers called me the following week to congratulate us on a fabulous concept and superb execution. In typical Hollywood fashion, each of the show's producers called to say how glad he or she was that they had thought of the fashion show.

We were a hit! So much so, in fact, that a year later this little last minute "stunt" morphed into the catalyst for the "Nolan Miller Dynasty Fashions" line, which was pre-sold into a national chain of clothing stores for an unprecedented, multi-million-dollar deal.

This was the real Dynasty bullion.

Chapter Four

MIAMI LICE

You can have the best show and the greatest cast.
But if your time slot is lousy, no one will ever know it.
You'll be cancelled before the season ends.

Some television aficionados go so far as to say that *Miami Vice* was the most influential television series of all time. It's remembered for being a huge hit right out of the gate. Sorry to burst that bubble, but that couldn't be further from the truth.

The show's genesis came in the form of a memo Brandon Tartikoff, then head of NBC, sent to *Hill Street Blues* producer and writer Anthony Yerkovich, requesting that Tony create a pilot script for a *concept* which Brandon referred to as "MTV Cops."

Yerkovich wrote the two-hour pilot script for *Miami Vice*. This alone made it a saleable beginning. Then the acclaimed film writer, producer, and director Michael Mann stepped in to direct the pilot and kidnapped the series from Yerkovich. The pilot was a culmination of Michael's new-wave artistic vision, Miami's mixed-race culture and music, the Art Deco look of South Beach, the pastels of the Miami skyline, neon lights flashing on Collins Avenue, and pink flamingos of course.

I was still slaving industriously on the Spelling account, when a call came from Universal Television's Executive Black Tower. They were re-questing that the Rogers & Cowan television flacksters take a look at this new drama and then put together an "innovative" marketing plan for it. Non-traditional is the term they stressed. They hoped we'd understand what they were looking for when we saw the pilot.

The series was cutting edge for its time. It had pulsing music, a siz-zling new look, and an eye-candy lead actor in Don Johnson (DJ). Ouch! Dressed in pastel T-shirts, white linen pants, Armani style jackets, loafers with no socks, sporting a perfect, two-day stubble, blond streaked hair, moves sychronized to a Jann Hammer score and stretched behind the wheel of a Testarossa....oh my gosh! Depending on your age, the character Sonny Crockett was a modern day Sheik, a new Valentino, or just plain Miami HOT.

Luck played the biggest roll in getting the semi-washed up druggie DJ cast as Sonny. Not the first or probably second choice for the role, he'd won it by default after Nick Nolte declined to make the move from movies to television.

The blond, tan and cool Sonny Crockett partnered with Ricardo Tubbs, played by Philip Michael Thomas, a snazzy black newcomer to television. Although the show ran a long while, Philip was never quite able to garner the attention DJ did.

DJ was already a Hollywood veteran. He starred in an early 70's film called *A Boy And His Dog* which over the next decade became somewhat of a cult classic. DJ was married to and divorced from Melanie Griffith, entered rehab more than once for recreational drug and alcohol use. He also portrayed Elvis Presley in a critically panned, television movie-of-the-week.

DJ was an old pro with the press. He knew exactly how to play the game. Poor Philip Michael Thomas (PMT), on the other hand, gave the impression he'd just gotten off the bus and tripped onto Sunset Boulevard. During NBC's fall lineup press junket, PMT greeted every reporter with his motto, "EGOT." This stood for, Emmy, Grammy, Oscar and Tony. "Someday I will win them all," he boasted to everyone within hearing range. I tried to make him realize his boastfulness could easily turn him into a Hollywood joke, but he never learned when to shut up.

Having initiated this potential ratings monster, Brandon slotted his concept for Friday nights at ten o'clock against CBS's ratings powerhouse *Dallas*. I criticized this decision calling it "a mistake of epic proportions." It turned out this bravado move damn near killed off our show.

I was first introduced to our future megastars at a studio luncheon meet and greet. There is nothing more mortifying than to be trapped at a lunch with a handful of deeply mistrusted and dull television studio executives. Our two hip, young actors made it clear they would rather be anywhere else. Actors are squirmy to begin with. DJ and PMT appeared to have a severe case of the crabs.

I sat quietly eating my leafy greens while each MALE exec gave the boys the old up and down, "We're excited...masterful performances...cutting edge..."

As the bullshit was winding down, one of the studio suits introduced me. "This is Sally of Rogers & Cowan who we've brought on to handle you...I mean handle your P.R."

Ha! Ha! Back slaps all around. Good one Joe! "Take it away Sally."

I gazed into two totally blase' faces, knowing perfectly well what they were thinking. Their brains were on overdrive mulling over whom exactly they would hire as their personal publicist just as soon as they established their territory. Perhaps the publicist who handled De Niro? My ace in the hole was that I knew neither had the green or the juice for that move just yet. Right now I was the only game in town, so they'd better play nice with me in the sandbox, at least for a while.

"So gentlemen," I began. "I hear you're going out to the firing range this afternoon to learn how to shoot guns like real cops."

"Yeah, so?" DJ was testy.

"It just so happens I know how to shoot pretty damn well. Want me to come along and demonstrate some real action for you?"

"Yeah sure, sister." DJ was into his Sonny Crockett cockiness, but I could tell he was intrigued.

I rode with DJ, who drove me bananas, because he was a chain smoker and I don't imbibe. Still, I learned some useful things about him. DJ lived in Santa Monica with an actress by the name of Patti D'Arbanville, who was Cat Steven's ex-old lady and his motivation for the hit song, *My Lady D'Arbanville*. Patti and DJ had a child together named Jesse and an adopted dog named Jones. DJ was, he assured me, drug and alcohol free. For years he'd been a coke sniffer backed by booze chasers. His dog's name served as a reminder that he used to bear the weight of a "jones" on his back. Unfortunately, he'd earned an industry reputation for wrecking a hotel room or two. People warned me to watch out for this guy.

It was a long ride. When we finally pulled over I had no idea where we ended up. Some place in Ventura County way north of the Studio.

'SHOOTER AT ELEVEN O'CLOCK...TWO...NINE."

The shooting instructor had the guys spinning, cocking, taking aim, shooting, and...missing. Not one shot hit the target. It was painfully obvious these guys not only had to learn to hit the target, but also how to keep from getting dizzy as they spun around.

Fortunately, the instructor did not invite me to demonstrate my marksmanship abilities. So my mastery in the art remained unchallenged. The truth is, I'd just been playing the guys for effect. I couldn't shoot a water gun and hit the side of a barn if my life depended on it.

Nothing like a little *yarn* to get the action going I always say. I had learned in Hollywood if you are going to play a role, play it convincingly. Fib.

Soon dummy bullets were whizzing everywhere. It really hurts when you get hit by one. So I wisely ducked behind the wall along with the instructor who confided to me, "This is fucking hopeless. I vote for stunt men."

On the drive home I learned DJ was two years older than me. These days when I come across an updated bio for him it seems he is now two or more years younger. My goodness. One of us should have paid more attention in math class.

The week before the series debut I flew to Miami to spend time with the production unit in an effort to soothe any taut nerves. The roll of the Dade County Police Department Captain had been recast after the pilot was shot, because the producers felt they needed more heat in the roll. They got plenty of heat to spare in the form of Mr. Zoot Suit himself, the incomparable Hispanic actor, Edward James Olmos. This, however, kicked off a neurosis through the cast as to who'd be replaced next. I was on hand to calm the troubled waters, but was pleasantly surprised that everyone seemed to be getting along perfectly. DJ was in a fine mood. His girlfriend Patti was visiting and joined the cast members at a Miami Dolphins' game.

Not wanting to waste a public appearance, I had the bunch of us make a grand entrance at the stadium via speedboat with DJ himself pilot-

*Sally and Don took lots of boat trips. Sally is in the
center (fifth from the right), and Don Johnson is
sitting up front (third from the right).*

ing. He may not know how to shoot worth a damn, but he could certainly
hit a dock.

After the game we sped back across the water to a trendy beachside
restaurant for dinner. While enjoying the beautiful evening, DJ noticed
I was gazing at a really handsome man seated across the patio. He whispered to me, "I know he's good looking, but he's also the biggest drug
dealer in Miami." Even I knew that meant BIG.

My boss at Rogers & Cowan heard I was having a good time in
Miami, so he assumed my work was done and called me home. I asked
to stay at least awhile longer for the after-debut party, but he refused. It
was a stupid move on his part. I was making headway with this difficult
bunch, nurturing a trust that would prove invaluable in the months to
come. Even DJ was agreeing to be agreeable. That alone was a miracle.

I heard the debut after-party was terrific, but our initial ratings tanked. CBS swept the night with *Dallas*. It looked like my hunch was unfortunately playing out. We were depressed.

NBC had run a solid month of prime-time promotional spots leading up to our debut, and we still flopped. As a result I couldn't get arrested pitching stories about the show or interviews with the stars with regional press, let alone national publications. I decided to call in a big chit I'd been saving for a crisis. A writer for People Magazine owed me a favor. He hesitantly agreed to pay up by committing to a one-page black and white feature story on DJ for a November issue.

Nevertheless, our client Universal Television was not very happy with the Rogers & Cowan team's performance and called a crisis meeting. We were floundering through this conference when suddenly I had an *epiphany.* To the horror of my co-workers, I hijacked the floor. "We aren't going to get anywhere with our campaign until the regular season ends in February, and *Dallas* reruns begin." I continued on with my train of thought consciously projecting a well thought-out agenda (even though I was winging it).

"We will make no further attempts at garnering significant ink (the "in" lingo for press) until reruns begin. Then when the timing is right, we'll be ready with a media blitz the likes of which has never been seen." With an air of sincere conviction in my voice, I explained that we needed time to educate the press on the new *Miami Vice* look.

"They aren't getting it yet. They need time to catch up," I declared.

On the long ride back to the office, I half expected Rogers & Cowan to fire me, or for Universal to fire the lot of us. But since no one had come up with anything better, I became the go-to girl.

We hung out by the water coolers, and hung on by our fingernails until the timing was right. Then, in February, as promised, we began the carefully prepared media blitz, breaking loose all over the place. *New York Magazine* ran a ten-page photo spread, the *Miami Vice* cast was emblazoned on the cover of People, personal appearances were booked on *The Tonight Show,* and well...you name it, we nailed it!

My hunch turned out to be right on the money. The press needed time to discover *Miami Vice.* When we backed off and gave them time to catch up, they pushed our show in a big, big way!

To help us prepare for our blitz, Michael Mann hired an obscure but very talented photographer named Gusmano Cesaretti who magnificently captured "the *Miami Vice* look". These shots were edgy and dangerous. One memorable photograph was taken in an old St. Croix cemetery. It showed pastel linens flowing out from behind decaying graves holding modern semi-automatic weapons. When we finally convinced a few major publications to print these photographs, it was a major leap forward for mainstream press worldwide.

To his credit, Brandon Tartikoff stuck to his plan and kept *Miami Vice* on Friday nights, even though many thought he should bail. It would take a whole year, but *Miami Vice* finally topped the ratings and unseated *Dallas.* I told Brandon the next time he hit the Vegas tables I wanted to be right next to him. His bet paid off and in a BIG way. I had developed a deep admiration for Brandon during our *Miami Vice* adventures. It was a fondness and respect that lasted until his premature death in 1997, when at the age of forty-eight, he died of Hodgkin's disease. He was a good guy, the real deal.

Miami Vice was on the media's radar now. The producers began to fight for credit. Yerkovich and Mann went at it. Each wanted credit for this hit. I began to duck and weave to avoid being hit by the verbal farts they launched at each other.

A real "coup" came when Jann Wenner, publisher of *Rolling Stone Magazine,* broke his own longstanding rule and decided to feature a television show on the cover. Legendary photographer Annie Liebovitz was employed to shoot this unprecedented photo, but fell ill at the last moment. A talented but lesser-known female photographer stood in. While attempting to do her job, this poor woman apparently took a great deal of abuse from DJ. I received an urgent call from the set indicating that our photographer had broken down in tears. Not hard to believe. DJ could lash out, intimidate, and humiliate a person. To deal with him, you needed to wear a bullet-proof attitude. I learned to put mine on whenever I was around him.

Once the show took off, so did DJ's ego. It sailed totally out of control.

For months we had been advertising appearances by our two new stars at the *National Radio* promotion party in Miami. On the eve of the February event, PMT grew pissy and became mysteriously "ill". He was hospitalized and missed attending. Rumors flew. Had he overdosed? Had he suffered a nervous breakdown? The *Star* sent their most aggressive reporter to crash the event. He did his utmost to intimidate me by pinning me into a corner and bullying me into admitting that PMT was in rehab for an overdose.

Even if it was true, I would never have "admitted" anything. But to this day I have no idea why PMT was in the hospital. If he was in the hospital, I doubt it was for drugs. *Miami Vice* was filmed in some seedy and filthy locations, and so I suspect PMT picked up a case of hepatitis or something similar on set. But it was extremely unlikely his "illness" was caused from shooting anything with a needle.

Whatever the truth was, I wasn't about to put up with some nasty booger from a sleazy tabloid threatening me, so I called over my new best friend, Big Boy the bodyguard, and had the asshole bodily removed from the premises.

I just love those big ol' bodyguards. They do come in so handy.

PMT's no-show put DJ into a snit, and he decided not to show up at the party either. Three months prior he would have been eager to attend the opening of an envelope. But now, this kind of blatant publicity stunt was apparently beneath him and he would have no part of it. Beneath him maybe, but his no-show became front-page fodder for the tabloids the next day.

Although he had missed the party, DJ, suffering from a lack of attention, condescended to attend the private dinner later that evening. He sat across from me refusing to eat anything but prawns. I marveled how he managed to swallow so many of the tasty crustaceans when he was so full of himself already.

I visited DJ in his trailer on my way to the airport the next day.

"You know," I said quietly, "You need to remember something. What goes up inevitably comes down."

Back in LA a few weeks later, I rode out to the airport to personally greet DJ at LAX. He was appearing on *The Tonight Show,* and I was his escort for the evening. I picked him up in *The Tonight Show's* guest black limo. When we arrived at NBC Burbank, we learned that Johnny Carson was ill. Comedian David Brenner would be subbing for Johnny that night. DJ went ballistic! He bounced off the walls. I dragged him into his dressing room trying to calm him down. But he was out of control, loudly tossing out insulting remarks and savage threats.

Although in tantrum mode, he still agreed to go on. We were escorted into the TV set and seated in the audience section to watch the rehearsal. Still fuming, DJ suddenly turned to me and said, "Sally, you know everything about me, but I don't know anything about you." It wasn't a question really, more of a statement.

"Let's keep it that way shall we," I replied. There was no way I was delving into anything personal with this guy.

DJ planned to meet two friends for dinner after *The Tonight Show* taping. I asked our driver to drop me at my office and offered DJ the limo for the rest of the evening.

"I don't want your limo. I want a bigger one," he whined, sounding like a three-year-old.

"Why?" I asked. "The limo holds six."

"It isn't big enough," he exclaimed. "I don't want to be seen in it. I want a stretch limo!"

Dear God, I thought. Look what we've unleashed.

Over the next year *Miami Vice* morphed into a genuine phenomenon and the stars' egos gathered steam. They rolled over anyone in their way—fast and furiously.

Fortunately for me, I got a wonderful opportunity to move out of their way for good. Steven Spielberg offered me a job working for *Amblin Entertainment* handling his new NBC television anthology series, *Amazing Stories.* I left Rogers & Cowan. This was a good move for me, and I was fortunate to have Brandon Tartikoff at NBC still covering my ass.

Amblin did not just offer me another job, but a totally new environment. I had only been there for two weeks when my new secretary alerted me that Don Johnson was on the phone. I picked up.

"You walked out on me you bitch!" the words tumbled out of him.

"No, DJ." I remained cool. "I didn't walk out on anyone. I left Rogers & Cowan. I never worked for you. I was representing the show."

"I don't like people who leave me," was the last thing he said to me and hung up.

It was interesting that as long as I'd been around DJ, he never attempted to replace me with a personal publicist. I'd helped him form media relationships. I set up all his press, and handheld when necessary. I worked similarly with Eddie Olmos as well, but made it clear I represented the *series* not the individual actors.

Nevertheless, I was about to find out just how pissed off DJ was at me for what he felt was a desertion.

Three or four months into *Miami Vice's* third season, press began to insinuate that the show glamorized drug use. This kind of perception, spurred on by the press's insatiable hunger for a good story, wasn't good PR for the studio or the network. As a result, Lew Wasserman, CEO of MCA (parent company of Universal) was not a happy camper. He wanted something done to change this perception, and quickly.

He suggested that DJ cut an anti-drug promotional spot for television and theater distribution, demographically targeting teenagers.

When Lew Wasserman made a "suggestion" he expected it to be done.

At this time, word was DJ was wreaking havoc in Miami. He'd hired Elliot Mintz, a media advisor, which is a pompous ass term for publicist. It was hard to figure out who was most full of himself: DJ or Mintz. Mintz's claim to fame was he handled Yoko Ono. I believe he has since left the business completely, worn out by his last client, Paris Hilton.

Although I worked full-time with Amblin, I agreed to ferry Wasserman's request personally to DJ in Miami. I booked a direct flight for the following Sunday night, but then learned that DJ was actually in LA for the weekend staying at the Hotel Bel-Air. Fabulous. I reached him there and asked if I might drop by for a minute to tell him about a spot Lew Wasserman wanted him to do.

feature page

Kissing and telling about that hunk Don Johnson

Johnson: Puckered up   Dunaway: Moving

Ben was at the table of nominee, Angela ("Murder She Wrote") Lansbury. I was a table away with Barbara Stanwyck, who was this year's recipient of the Cecil B. DeMille award for meritorious service to films. And maybe three tables away was nominee Don Johnson, who later won the Golden Globe for best actor in a TV series.

There's so much written about TV's current H-O-T star, Johnson — some good, some not so good. That all comes with the territory of stardom. Well if ever anyone tells you, or you read that Don Johnson is not polite, don't you believe it.

Comfortably seated at his table he immediately, as a gentleman, stood up to greet us, as we shook hands. Then when he told Don, "Shirley is a friend of Sally Van Slyke's," Johnson smiled broadly, leaned over and

... Slyke was the ...publicist for "Mi... Universal with ...Amazing Stories." ...leman Don John... ...ort of ...them ...rls w ...to thump-thump-thump at the ... the name, "Don Johnson."

This was my first time a Globes. I can't get over the num who show up for these awards given out by a rather small gro wood-based foreign correspon write about the American min industries.

It's a much more relaxed than at the Oscars, possibly becau cocktail hour first, then dinner, TV show on which the awa nounced.

and we shook hands. Then when he told Don, "Shirley is a friend of Sally Van Slyke's," Johnson smiled broadly, leaned over and kissed me on the cheek. Van Slyke was the original Rogers & Cowan publicist for "Miami Vice." She's now at Universal with Steven Spielberg and his "Amazing Stories."

Sally, even though gentleman Don Johnson's peck on my cheek sort of belongs to you, I'll keep it for a while, then pass it along

on St. Valentine's Day, and that's the tr Faye Dunaway, in a shimmering g sleeveless beaded gown, told us during c tall hour that she's moving back to the from London where she and husband, O'Neill, have lived for several years. that she's reading a lot of feature m scripts, hoping to find one she really l Who said it wouldn't last? Married a two months, now, Joan Collins and Holm are still smooching and holding h Well they were anyway at the Globes Collins' CBS-TV mini-series, "Sins" 8 (Channel 2 in Detroi "You are committed, because last spring you while we were filmi about the table behavi actress, and Golden C the TV show. She v kept shouting her ap gers and presenters o nd songs. ositive shouting, but and annoying. The were embarrassed. wonderful. Her off this night, was loud, ut of order.

DJ curtly explained he was sorry, but he didn't have any time to meet this weekend and would be flying back to Miami Sunday night via private plane. So I asked if I might hop on the flight with him and we could talk then. I would catch a commercial flight back to LAX later.

No way. He would meet with me in Miami on Monday. I was to call his assistant for the time and location.

Okay. I got it. I had to play his game. I flew American Airlines into Miami on Sunday night. Bright and early Monday morning I called to schedule the meeting and was told DJ would not have time to meet with me until Thursday or Friday. He was on set until then and too busy.

Okay. I got it—message received again. Now it was time to make sure he got it.

I requested a production car to drive me out to the set. They were shooting that day on a local beach that was privatized for the shoot. When I arrived, I asked to see the day's call sheet. DJ's name was on it, so he was sure to be on set. I walked down the beach towards the crew setting up the next shot. I spotted DJ sitting with his back to me. As I headed towards him, two gentlemen stepped up to block my way.

"Hi, I'm Sally," I began," and I'm here to see DJ. It will just take a second."

"Mr. Johnson will not be able to see you at this time," the hulkiest of the two replied.

Then PMT appeared and joined DJ. Laughing loudly, PMT stage whispered, "They sent Sally down to make it happen, man. They be pulling out the big guns. You know you can't turn Miss Sally Van Slyke down." He high fived DJ.

The entire company was now staring at me. Their revered co-actor and my friend Eddie Olmos suddenly appeared and walked over to his two co-stars. I have no idea what he said, but I witnessed the body language which was loud and clear. PMT went silent. DJ didn't move. Neither said another word.

Next, Eddie walked over to me. He gave me a kiss hello and apologized for DJ's rudeness. "Let's go talk to Don," he suggested.

But you know what? It was too late. I'd had my fill and wasn't willing to subject myself to more of their demeaning bullshit.

"I'm out of here, Eddie," I told him.

"I can't blame you," he replied. "They have short memories."

He put his arm around me and together we walked slowly off the beach. When I got to the car the phone was ringing. Back at the hotel, the phone continually rang as I packed my bags. As I left the hotel, there was a message at the front desk that I refused to pick up. I left Miami. Fuck it. This mess was no longer my problem.

Later, I heard through the grapevine that Lew Wasserman was very displeased to hear that DJ had blown off his emissary. Lew owned and operated the telescope that kept a close watch on Universal's galaxy of many stars. It was no coincidence that after my Miami trip Don Johnson's star began to dim. His career never really became the bright light Don expected it to be.

Funny how things work in Hollywood.

Chapter Five

JAWS THE REVENGE

Many sequels drift out to sea. Others never make it to shore.

While on the job as a daily assignment reporter at Metromedia, I caught a Sunday matinee of *Jaws,* directed by Steven Spielberg. Joining me in playing hooky was my ex-cop cameraman Rex. The Hose, as we liked to call him, was tough. He could leap barbed wire fences in a single bound while being chased by a bevy of gun slinging bodyguards just to "get the story." I was the reporter who brought up, and more than once covered, his rear.

This particular Sunday afternoon we were on news story standby ready to race at a moment's notice to cover whatever breaking story might arise. It wasn't looking like this was likely to happen any time soon, so why not slide into a movie theater? After all, if the assignment desk needed us all they had to do was page. So after doling out the cost of a matinee ticket and purchasing popcorn, we traveled to the fictional island town of Amity, ready for an adventure.

Everyone who saw *Jaws* will remember the young blond girl, not a care in the world, laughing while she dove into the tranquil moonlit ocean for a romantic midnight swim. Then the shark entered to the memorable sound of a chelloed heartbeat, growing louder and closer. First the jerking motions. Then the screams for help. Finally, complete silence.

Slam cut.

A close-up of Amity's Chief of Police, played by Roy Scheider, staring out at the water. "What happened here?" By God, he would find out as this mystery unfolded. The Hose, on the other hand, didn't care to find out. He attempted to race for the exit. I had to grab him by his rainbow boxers and haul him back into his seat.

"Have we been paged?" I asked.

"No," was the short answer.

I asked again, "Do you have a bathroom emergency?"

"No," he repeated.

I was confused. So what was his problem? He wasn't saying. But when we had our first real sighting of the shark, the Hose was so startled at this terrible visage he tossed his extra butter popcorn across several rows in front of us and ducked his head under the seat.

"Tell me when it's over!"

I couldn't believe it. The old Hose was downright terrified. This brave leaper of fences remained on the floor for most of the movie.

"What's happening now?" he whispered. "Sshhhhh!," I answered back.

I loved Jaws. Bruce the Shark, as he was later nicknamed, certainly had extraordinary powers of analytical thinking for a fish.

The Hose, on the other hand, suffered for weeks from nightmares where sharks chased him in the studio parking lot.

A huge blockbuster success, *Jaws* and Bruce now belonged to the special hall of fame known as sequel madness—the life-blood of the movie business. If one works you can be sure there will be "too many" sequels to follow. Somehow I managed to miss Jaws II and III. Spielberg didn't direct either one, and the reviews were fishy to poor. Number three took place in a tourist water park tunnel. Bruce took a wrong turn in this incredibly convoluted script and the reviews were buried at sea.

Even though the sequels were getting progressively worse, Hollywood can never say enough is enough. So here comes *Jaws IV: The Revenge*. At this time I was hired on at Universal Pictures. This picture would be my first foray into the challenging world of film marketing. Little did I know I was about to be flung, still wet behind the ears, into the deep end of Amity Harbor.

I first met the new president of marketing, a lovely gay man named Ed Roginski, at a Thanksgiving dinner hosted by a dear friend of mine.

I liked him immediately, and over the course of the next few months we built up a strong rapport.

When I arrived on scene at Universal Pictures, I wasn't aware that Ed was shoving my hire down The Chairman's throat. The Chairman did not want Ed to give me the job. He fought the idea for weeks, repeating over and over to Ed, "She just isn't a *player*. All she knows is television."

However, Ed insisted on an interview and forced The Chairman to meet me for breakfast with the hope that I would be able to defrost the apparent chill he had towards me.

We met bright and early at the Universal Hilton cafe. That, in itself, was a big hint I wasn't welcome. If he was seriously interested in meeting me, he would have scheduled a *power breakfast* at the Beverly Hills Hotel Polo Lounge. To make the situation even more uncomfortable than it already was, The Chairman brought along his sidekick, the president of production.

They worked in tandem to be incredibly rude and condescending. Half the time they ignored me completely, talking hush-hush inside jargon to each other. When they deemed to ask me a question it was with complete disinterest. When I explained I'd been a television reporter, The Chairman commented I must not have been very good at it or I'd still be on air. Yes, I was working currently for Steven Spielberg handling his new television anthology series, but "any idiot could sell television," came the insult flung in my direction.

At long last I was excused from the table and left this grueling session ready to call a shrink. At least I had not yet given notice and still had a good job that "any idiot" could do. Maybe I didn't want in to this exclusive league after all.

To make matters worse, I did not hear back from Ed Roginski. So imagine my surprise when on a Monday morning three weeks later he finally called and offered me a three-year contract. Stunned, my first reaction was to turn down the job. I explained to Ed what had transpired at the breakfast. I described the duo as "complete shits."

"No doubt," Ed went on to explain, "That was done deliberately to see how and if you can take the pressure. I hear you did okay."

Then he spent the next hour talking me into accepting the job. Of course I did. I was now the Vice President of West Coast Publicity for Universal Pictures. And now meant RIGHT NOW. No two weeks notice.

The very next day I attended my first Tuesday production/marketing meeting. The topic at hand was the upcoming release of *Jaws IV: The Revenge* directed by Joseph Sargent and starring Michael Caine. Actress Lorraine Gary would reprise her Jaws I roll, this time as the widow of Amity's chief of police. *An important political side note:* Lorraine Gary was also married in real life to MCA Universal's CEO and second in command, Sid Sheinberg.

Suddenly The Chairman turned to me—we hadn't spoken since our breakfast—and asked me how I planned to publicize the film. I wanted to say, "How the hell do I know? I just got here." But I wisely fell on my sword and kept quiet.

"Can't you talk?" Is what I believe he queried before ignoring me again and moving forward with the meeting. On his way out, however, he loudly whispered to Ed for all to hear, "See, she doesn't know anything."

Let me tell you what I did know. It was something even The Chairman did not know, and would not know for many months. I alone knew Ed Roginski had recently been diagnosed with full-blown AIDS. How I knew this will remain a secret until I die. Ed had not told me. The point is...I knew. So I desperately wanted to come through big time for Ed, because he believed in me. He needed me to take some of the pressure off him. I made a vow to myself that, so help me God, I would do just that.

The next Tuesday I went to the weekly marketing meeting fully prepared with a plan for the *Jaws IV* premiere. It was a press stunt I knew The Chairman would love. I wasn't going to start the new position treading water, so I took control. I informed everyone we would hold the premiere of the film at a hugely popular Orange County waterslide park. Guests would watch the movie while swimming immersed in the giant pool complete with a wave machine. The press and guest giveaway package would contain fins, a snorkel, a T-shirt and a towel in the shape of Bruce. "Can't you just hear the screams now?" I asked, staring straight at The Chairman.

Bingo! I was The Chairman's hero of the moment. He loved this kind of crap. "Set it up now," he enthused. "It's a fucking genius idea."

In fact, it was a great idea—until we previewed the movie.

With the opening scene, my short-lived movie career life began to flash in front of my eyes. Lorraine Gary turned directly into the camera for a close-up, and I swear the entire audience groaned. She looked absolutely terrible. Old and worn out. Definitely in need of some serious surgical help.

Michael Caine was the proverbial fish out of water. He was so completely miscast it would have been funny if so much hadn't been riding on his performance. He flopped around in the water in such a way that it appeared as though he really didn't know how to swim. Fortunately, he spent very little time in the water. Otherwise he'd have drowned for sure, even before the shark got to him.

Director Joseph Sargent shot the picture primarily on the man-made lake at Universal's Backlot and it looked that way. Bruce the shark appeared to have been embalmed one too many times. He looked like a cheap plastic toy from a cereal box and was enhanced by antiquated very un-special effects.

As the screening played on, all I could see were the headlines the morning after our scheduled water park premiere: *"Bruce takes one dive too many! "* or *"Chaos erupted during last night's world premiere of Jaws IV: The Revenge, as hundreds of screaming swimmers fought to escape the total boredom! "*

The entire marketing department agreed. We had to cancel this premiere at the eleventh hour and eat the cost. Even The Chairman cut me some slack and agreed without a snit. The best promotion idea was NO promotion now—or ever. Suck it up and smile. After all, none of us had any doubt that the Hall of Shame would award *Jaws IV: The Revenge* the honor of being named one of the top-ten worst pictures of all time.

It was.

Chapter Six

DRAGNET

Dum-de-dum-dum!

*"This is the city. Hollywood, California. 6:00 PM.
We headed west on the boulevard of dreams..."*

Dragnet, Universal's new comedy spoof based on the Jack Webb television series, starred Tom Hanks and Dan Aykroyd and promised to be the summer's blockbuster. Our two detectives emboldened the cover of *Premiere* magazine. So it was no surprise to me when The Miller Brewing Company and MTV wanted to tie in with us and were willing to spend megabucks to do so.

We, and by "we" I mean me, put *my* head together and came up with the idea of airing the first ever live MTV broadcast of a Hollywood premiere hosted by Universal Studios and the Miller Brewing Company. At first this sounded like a perfect idea! I should have known there were no perfect ideas in Hollywood, just plenty of perfectly huge Hollywood egos.

Even so, I commanded my amazing promotion department team to "get it together," and they did. I loved working with these guys; they really knew their stuff and the planning went smoothly (or so I thought).

A week before the premiere, we were set to screen the finished picture in New York City. I flew in on the red-eye, dreaming about the accolades I was sure to get from our sponsors. In New York, I joined the MTV and Miller executives along with a few hundred wide-eyed, regular moviegoers for what promised to be a fun evening. As the lights dimmed in the theater, the excitement was palpable.

The movie did not disappoint. As expected, there was much merriment, sustained laughter, and thunderous applause. As the credits rolled, I saw a few hundred smiling faces emerge from the dark, followed by the

Miller execs who, rather than smiling, looked like they had just witnessed an execution. I thought it might be mine. They closed in on me.

"How could you do this to us?" one Hopster scoffed right in my face.

I was flummoxed, but stammered out, "Do? Do what exactly?"

"Did you people think you could get away with it?" another spat.

"Get away with what exactly?" I began inching backwards, feeling my way towards the exit. What had they seen?

In a 106-minute movie, jam packed with Miller beer logos, there was a less-than-one-minute scene where Sergeant Friday is interrogating a buxom contortionist stripper in a sleazy downtown bar. Suddenly she doubles back, head framed between her thighs, and gazes seductively back at him. The lens zooms in through her legs, focusing on the background bar action. This is what most people saw anyway.

But the Miller execs spied a giant florescent *Bud Lite* sign framed in the center of two perfectly-honed gams.

I must have blinked, because I missed it as did everyone else. The Miller execs saw only the *Bud Lite* sign and threatened to pull the plug on the whole live premiere right then and there. The solution came in the form of an ointment usually used on diaper rash. After much bellyaching from the director and producers, the editor agreed to "smear" the guilty frames with Vaseline Petroleum Jelly. The *Bud Lite* sign was miraculously transformed into a hazy red blob on this celluloid baby.

Problem solved. Only a couple of casualties: one pissed off director and a seething editor.

A week later, the night of the premiere was a crystal clear evening perfect for viewing the stars. The police closed Hollywood Boulevard to all but foot traffic. The live broadcast would begin with a six-block-long parade, led by none other than the USC Trojan Marching Band and followed by a fleet of 1950s convertibles ferrying the filmmakers and lesser stars. Tom Hanks was behind the wheel of a vintage police car dandily dressed in a 50s suit and hat. Dan Aykroyd, in his leathers, was set to bring up the rear, skidding in on his Harley "da hog" with his wife Donna

Dixon hanging off the rear, playing the part of his biker bitch to perfection.

Several of my field staff were stationed at the parade starting gate, charged with moving all the players out in order and on time. I was on hand to greet them as they arrived at the door to the theater. The budget, already stretched, did not include the new headsets I had requested. So we would have to coordinate our efforts via the existing old headsets that made everything sound like you were driving through a tunnel. "Crackle. Crackle. What did you say???"

Both sides of the street were jammed with fans and other colorful localites. News crews moseyed around shooting B-roll and basking in catcalls.

At 6 pm straight up, the USC marching band kicked off with a sound cue:

Dum-de-dum-dum!

The crowd mimicked, "Dum-de-dum-dum....dum!" We were now live and rolling.

Crackle, crackle... "What did you say?" My earpiece must have malfunctioned again, because I thought I heard someone say, "Dan's hog was swiped!" Ridiculous! "Repeat that again?"

It seemed some felonious lookie-loo had made off with "da hog" right under Sgt. Friday's very nose.

"Quick," I screamed into the static. " Get A-Aykroyd into H-Hanks's car."

"What Sally? S----mmzzz...doommm? Can't heearrr uuuzz."

Too late. Hanks was already rolling.

Dum-de-dum-dum!

6:05 pm. My partners and I were in the crapper now.

Hanks rolled into sight, his black and white jumping over the curb, belching and backfiring — all on cue. The crowd went wild. Tom, in character, toppled out the car door, stumbled over the running board and fumbled his way over to the MTV's D.J. host. It was perfect!

The crowd loved this. As Tom basked in the tumultuous howls, I sidled as inconspicuously as I could up to him and whispered in his ear, "Punt."

"Why?"

"Because 'da hog' got swiped and apparently Danny's walking in."

"Oh shit!" For a spit second Tom looked like a deer caught in headlights.

Hanks is a genuinely nice guy. Furthermore, he takes direction well and loves improv. Staying in character, he dove smack into the crowd, falling over his feet, handcuffs out and ready.

"Hey lady," he grabbed a great-grandmother. "You're under arrest."

A young kid started to make a comment and Hanks interrupted him. "You...yeah you kid. Put a sock in it or you're heading downtown!"

Grabbing a woman's purse and dumping the contents out on the ground, Tom sputtered, "This sort of thing is illegal here, ma'am."

Then mercifully we all heard it. Zoom-zoom....putt...puttttt....puttttt. Our man Friday rode down the boulevard, straddling a mini, Pepto-Bismol-pink moped. Donna hung precariously off the cycle's rear-end as Aykroyd pedaled up, making it to the curb just as the engine conked out. But who cared? The crowd went ballistic. The pink moped fell over on its side, and Hanks proceeded to arrest Dan for littering. You couldn't even hear Dum De Dum Dum anymore over the roars of laughter.

The MTV executive producer pounded me on the back, shrieking hysterically to be heard above the cacophony of the crowd: "This is fucking great television. You're a genius!"

"I'm glad it worked so well," I said, mustering my most humble look.

James Belushi, who I adore but had not yet met, watched all this action from the stands. He was the last official guest to enter the theater. As he passed me, he muttered, "Nice save, Red."

"A Blues Brother's sister never lets you down," I replied.

When the screening was mercifully underway, I received a message that a Pinky Pusse, owner of the moped, was asking for the return of his ride and perhaps a little remuneration, as was customary for services rendered. With time on my hands until the after-party kicked in, I revved up the now famous "pink hog" and zig-zagged back up the boulevard in my evening attire until I located our good Samaritan.

I found Mr. Pusse, ensconced in a natty sequined fuchsia evening frock with coordinating four-inch platforms and a feather boa. A perfectly-coiffed, magenta beehive provided the finishing touch to this eye-catching look. He was industriously working his corner office.

Sputtering to a stop, I slid off his ride and introduced myself, thanked him profusely for saving my ass, and palmed him a generous amount of green.

He accepted my gratitude and the cash. "Any time, Sally. I'm my best with redheads!"

Chapter Seven

IMAGINE

If Opie and Mr. Wow-Wow are two names you
wouldn't expect to find on the Hollywood A-list,
then you don't know Hollywood.

Parenthood was the second picture from *Imagine Entertainment* released through Universal. It tells the story of the Buckmans, an all-American, dysfunctional, extended family. Its stellar cast includes Steve Martin and Dianne Wiest. Their performances were Academy Award caliber.

Director Ron Howard and producer Brian Grazer founded Imagine Entertainment. They were known to our marketing team as Opie (the good cop) and Mr. Wow-Wow (the bad cop). Ron will always be nostalgically remembered as Opie, Sheriff Andy's adorable son from the *Andy Griffith Show* and, of course, Fonzie's pal Richie Cunningham from *Happy Days.*

Now a successful box office director, Ron had already earned his place on the Hollywood A-list. Brian, a USC Film School graduate, met his future partner while producing pilots for Paramount. Brian was equally talented, but his personality cast him in the role of a duplicitous court jester. That isn't to say Brian's not a good producer. He definitely is. However, producers aren't generally known for being nice.

Brian, to whom everything is "Wow! Wow!" stands about five feet five inches. Although I have known many short people in my life, right off the bat I found Brian to be awfully "small" as well as short. He seemed to take great pride in being fractious, frantic, and obnoxious.

Truth is, talking to him was much like talking to a kid with chronic ADD (Attention Deficit Disorder). I just hated getting stuck alone with him. For instance, one day in the Boston Ritz Carlton lobby, I spied Brian heading my way. At the same time, I spotted Rod Stewart stepping out of the elevator. Without a moment's hesitation I ran over to Rod, greeting him as if he were a long-lost friend even though we had never met. I palmed him my business card, and pleaded with him, "Help me escape that little dwid over there."

Rod's gaze followed the nod of my head. Smart man, he glanced at my card, realized who I was, and immediately understood my intention. Placing his arm around my shoulders, he escorted me right out the front door. I think Rod Stewart is adorable. I would have shown my gratitude by singing a few bars of "Tonight's the Night," but his wife was right there. At least I made my escape with him.

On the heels of Parenthood's success, The Chairman went in hot pursuit of an exclusive multi-picture deal with *Imagine Entertainment*. The first movie under this new agreement would be *Dream Team* starring Michael Keaton. *Dream Team* is the story of a psychologist at a New Jersey sanitarium assigned to work with four whacko inmates. One day he decides they all would benefit from taking a field trip to Yankee Stadium. On the way out the door, he gives each one pocket money for treats on their outing. Off they go, but naturally all goes awry and the four looney-tooneys are unleashed on Manhattan. Michael Keaton plays a pathological liar with delusions of grandeur and is a riot in the role. Since his character is the "most normal" of the bunch, he becomes the unofficial leader of the group.

"Ah, it's great to be young and insane," he sniffs, as he's perched on the precipice of escape.

The Chairman wanted an ostentatious industry-wide premiere party in Los Angeles, not so much to give the picture a box office boost, but more to give his ego a boost. This new deal between Imagine and Universal was a real coup.

My team managed to accomplish both. *The Dream Team* premiere was entitled, "Play Ball." It was one of the most celebrated events we ever conceived. We re-created the movie in party form.

Staged adjacent to the *Cineplex Odeon* complex on top of the hill at Universal City (the popular tourist attraction City Walk stands there now) we duplicated the Manhattan and Bronx Street scenes leading to

Yankee Stadium. Three huge tents were erected representing Manhattan, the Bronx, and the stadium.

As the guests filed out of the *Cineplex* screening, tour guides handed each a map to the game and distributed movie pocket money redeemable for refreshments and other goodies along the way. The Screen Extra's Guild provided a bevy of look-a-like localites. They were dressed as Manhattan socialites, Bronx hookers, diehard Yankee Fans, pickpockets, and ticket hawkers. They ambled the streets, mingling right along with our guests.

Entering the borough of Manhattan at a recreated Madison and 5th Avenue, guests could purchase bouquets of flowers from colorful sidewalk stands and pretzels with mustard off grill carts. Gucci watches and designer sunglasses were being hocked in abundance. The East Side Manhattan Dinner Club hosted a full bar and cocktail buffet. A tuxedoed maitre'd promised, "All you can eat for just a buck!"

In the Bronx ("yo, how ya doin?") the guests perched on shop stoops and sidewalks devouring hundreds of Nathan's hotdogs and slices of Great Meatball's of Fire Pizza. Competition for business was furious. Hawkers on every corner touted, "Get your dog and ice cold beer here!" Others sold Yankee T-shirts complete with our *Dream Team* movie logo on the back.

As I stood at the entrance to our Yankee Stadium, I could almost hear the forty-year veteran Yankee broadcaster Phil Rizzuto exclaim, "Holy Cow!"

When guests arrived the ticket-takers were swamped. Once inside, the *fans* made their way through the stands and onto the Astroturf field. Strobes flashed a bright white light while the DJ laid down a kick-ass dance track. This guy was so adroit on the turntable he actually got a too-cool-for-anything group of Hollywood uptight industry snobs onto the dance floor.

Leading the pack in abandon was Michael Keaton himself, who kicked it up all night, dancing with just about everyone. The Vice President of Finance for Universal Pictures, usually a worry wart about spending any unnecessary money, was so overcome with enthusiasm (which we all know is tough for those accountant types) that she went berserk when

Mr. DJ, having fulfilled his two hour contract, was about to shut down the music.

"Oh no you don't!" she yelled flinging herself onto his protective batting cage like an orangutan in heat. "I'm the one paying for this, and I'm telling you to keep playing!"

Who knew upwardly mobile Hollywood insiders would be caught dead having such a good time, but they did. They managed to cash out all their "spending money." Donned in logo-emblazoned T-shirts under their jackets, and clutching bunches of fresh flowers, they now headed home totally exhausted. A normally slim-conscious crowd had eaten everything in sight. I swear I even saw a size zero or two actually chow down a Nathan's dog. It was an impressive way to kick off what would become a great association with *Imagine Entertainment.*

Or was that just my imagination?

The reviews were extremely positive. But with success comes the inevitable downside of letting it go to your head. Our Brian reveled in the phenomenal press—a little too much. One day he actually said to me that he now only had time to meet with the really great people.

Wow!

Now in fairness (and gosh I'm trying to be fair here) what I think he meant was people who could teach him something. For instance, Brian was very impressed when he learned I'd grown up next door to Dr. Edward Teller, the physicist generally recognized as the father of the hydrogen bomb. He asked if I could arrange for him to meet Dr. Teller.

Talk about an over-active ego! I couldn't fathom such a meeting. Wow! I mean really, WOW! Who could be more self-aggrandizing?

Never mind. Brian's ADD kicked in and he seemed to forget Dr. Teller. Next he set his sites on meeting the Queen of England. This lofty idea sprang into his frontal cortex when he discovered that our Washington D.C. *Backdraft* premiere and national junket (the film had been shot in D.C.) was taking place at the same time Her Majesty was visiting our nation's capitol. Wow!

Brian rang my room early the morning of Her Majesty's scheduled arrival. He wanted me to wangle him an invitation to meet The Queen, preferably that afternoon, because that would work best for his schedule.

Can you believe the audacity of this court jester? No? Well, here's the kicker.

I made a few calls, and it turned out, his request was NOT a problem!

My friend Senator George Mitchell, who was the senate majority leader, standing Constitutionally two heartbeats away from the presidency, was kind enough to arrange for Brian to attend the laying of the wreath ceremony at the Tomb of the Unknown Soldier. All foreign dignitaries, especially those representing countries that fought in World War II, participate in this tradition when on an official state visit to the United States. The ceremony would be followed by a brief reception for Her Majesty and the Duke of Edinburgh to greet the select group of invited guests in the Arlington House.

Brian was all set to meet the Queen, even on his time schedule.

Mr. Wow-Wow suddenly changed his mind, saying, "Whoa...it's way too hot today, man. Besides, I don't really want to go if I can't meet the Queen by myself. I mean, who are all those other people?"

At this point, killing him would be a service to mankind. However, there was not enough time to dispose of the body. Someone had to haul ass and make an apologetic appearance to her Majesty for his no-show. So off I went with a couple of staffers in tow.

Not to boast, but I'd met the Queen on several occasions before. The first time I greeted her was when the royal yacht Britannia sailed into San Pedro Harbor. Another time was when I attended a garden party at Buckingham Palace. It rained on both occasions. As we drove to Arlington Cemetery, I remember thinking that this time I'd be overcome by heat and humidity rather than rain.

It was such a muggy day in Washington that the guests at Arlington House were advised to remain inside until we heard the twenty-one gun salute signaling Her Majesty's arrival. At that point, we were to step out on to the portico, watch the ceremony, form a reception line and greet the Royal party as they came up the steps from the Tomb.

Perfect. We were all getting along famously when we heard boom-boom-boom.

Her Majesty had arrived.

Boom-boom-boom. The salute continued. Then a slightly more resonate boom-boom-boom of thunder echoed.

Dressed appropriately in pastel summer silks and linens we all obediently stepped outside just as the sky literally burst open with a torrential downpour, completely drenching us as if someone were dumping a huge bucket of water.

It's times like this I actually envy royals. Her Majesty, dressed head to tow in lilac, a particularly becoming color for her, remained perfectly dry under two umbrellas held gracefully for her by her ladies in waiting. Not one drop touched The Queen.

I, on the other hand, was dressed in pale yellow silk that stuck to me like a wet T-shirt. It took only seconds, and I looked like I needed a box of Cling Free and a mop. My au courant tangerine clutch began to bleed all over the front of my jacket, and my handmade Italian summer pumps emitted a distinctive squishing sound when I stepped forward to greet our honored guests. I bowed slightly. It is proper for an American to shake hands with Her Majesty, just not when it's dripping wet.

Queen Elizabeth travels with a very dashing (and that is the best word to describe him) Royal Equerry, or what Americans might call an executive aide. He is charming, self-effacing and witty. Formal greetings over, I was swamp-footing it out of Arlington House at top speed when I felt a presence nearby. Glancing to my right I was absolutely humiliated to find Mr. Unbelievable walking alongside me. How mortifying. This man actually looked like he just walked off the pages of Cinderella. Very tall, wearing Saville Row from head to foot, hair touched elegantly with silver, with beguiling blue eyes that don't miss a thing.

"Hello again" he said, charmingly acknowledging we had met before.

"Hello again," I replied and added, "If you laugh at me I promise I'll cry."

"Why ever would I laugh?" he retorted. "I've never once seen you dry."

"Oh shut up," I started to laugh. "Obviously, Her Majesty has put a hex on me."

"Or you on her," he winked and was gone.

Gone except for in my dreams.

I arrived back at the hotel in Georgetown, creating puddles as I entered the lobby. I found Brian ensconced in a corner, speaking loudly on a house phone, feet up on the antique desk in front of him.

Ignoring my peculiar condition "How was the Queen?" he asked.

"Lovely," I replied with a dignity one can only accomplish sopping wet. "But the strangest thing happened. She never asked about you."

"Wow!" Not cool.

Chapter Eight

ORDINARY BOB'S MILAGRO

Milagro in Spanish means miracle.
For this clunker of a film it was going to take one.

I suspect there aren't many women, or men for that matter, who wouldn't want to meet the man behind the face of such compelling characters as the Sundance Kid, Jay Gatsby and Hubbell Gardiner. All of these movie characters were portrayed by Robert Redford, or as we referred to him in Hollywood: Ol' Ordinary Bob.

For those playing it straight, the nickname is based on Redford's first Oscar which he won for directing the film, *Ordinary People.* For the rest of us, call it a metaphor for a mercurial enigma.

The day had begun resplendently. A brilliant sun rose in a cloudless sky over a drowsy Los Angeles summer morning. Ordinary Bob had requested a 7:00 in the morning meeting, although he did not arrive until 8:30, to discuss the potential marketing campaign for a picture he still hadn't finished directing. It had been two damn long years, and the picture was well over budget.

On his fantasy veranda, I listened as Ol' Bob painted a landscape of breathtaking colors, lavender green sagebrush, tall spires of blue grass wafting in the breeze, ochre adobe, and the rich sienna of earth. His mellifluous voice mesmerized me. I gazed spellbound into those famous azure eyes, perfectly framed by the famous tousled blonde mane. He gazed back. Was I having a romantic dream? A milagro?

"Oh snap out of it!" cautioned my alter ego.

His dulcet tones continued, "All I need is more time and a few location days to capture that one spectacular rainbow juxtaposed like perfect prose against the glorious pale southwestern sky."

It was time to stop dreaming and pay attention. I had mastered the art of appearing riveted while almost asleep, but I also knew how to wake up when someone insinuated the need for "more money." Ordinary Bob needed more money. The unfinished celluloid was sitting in the can raking up interest by the second. Like Bob, the film was late. Ordinary Bob was inordinately late for everything. He never offered apologies because, "ah shucks he's just Ordinary Bob."

Believe me it was a grande milagro con mucho dinero when Ordinary Bob finally got the finished picture in the can six months later.

His film *The Milagro Beanfield War* is a fable about a small, New Mexico farming village inhabited by an ephemeral guardian angel. Residents of this tiny hamlet are threatened by the evil hand of corporate greed. The ensemble cast includes Sônia Braga, Rubén Blades, Christopher Walken, and John Heard, all highly accomplished actors but nary a one popular enough to induce a stampede of paying patrons into local theaters.

I have always described the film, *Milagro,* as a too-long yet lyrically sweet picture rescued from oblivion by a fabulous original score composed by Dave Grusin who won an Oscar for this truly magical work. If you combine my own critique with professional reviews that began, "an interesting piece from Oscar winner" or "artistically adventurous" you'll get the drift.

The film was shot just outside of Santa Fe. So it made sense to hold the international press junket and premiere in Taco Bell City. We marketers thought this would be different, appropriate, fun, and most importantly—out of town.

Ordinary Bob promised to be on hand for the festivities which included an early afternoon Low Rider's contest, an evening screening, and an after-party staged at an adorable little Santa Fe adobe house where artist Georgia O'Keeffe died in 1984. Although compelling, the house is inconveniently located about ten miles out of town. It was currently owned by an oil millionaire whose female assistant fancied Ordinary Bob big time.

In today's politically correct world, a Low Rider's parade might be interpreted as blatant stereotyping. However, political correctness wasn't a household topic yet, and the City Council of Santa Fe voted to host the parade. Ordinary Bob agreed to show up and be the sole judge of the entrants' efforts. I conceded to stand alongside him on the platform and count the bouncing dice rolling by.

It was great fun. All the different old Chevy drives were weighted with sandbags in the trunk, sporting suicide doors and fenders so low they scraped the pavement causing sparks to fly. Many of the drivers were dressed in traditional Pachuco style, pinstripes and gold lame. Their old ladies had huge "dos" reminiscent of a young Priscilla Presley. They preened outrageously.

"Hey movie man...you like my cruise man?"

"Hey Sundance, you want to ride my chromes real low, slow and easy Ese?"

"Te Quiero, Senor!"

For once, Ordinary Bob seemed to be having a good time, too. He hemmed and hawed, but finally awarded the grand prize of four premiere tickets for the evening to the '58 Chevy Impala with a hand-painted mural of Butch Cassidy and the Sundance Kid on both sides. Santa Fe is chock full of good artists, and whoever painted this had real talent.

The premiere screening, slated for "roll em" at seven-thirty, was jam packed by five. State officials, City Council members, Tourist Bureau representatives, and everyone else of any note in town wanted to say a few words of welcome to Ordinary Bob. They meant well. The problem was they didn't seem to know the definition of a few words. Speeches droned on past eight-thirty. The Mayor, dressed colorfully in a beautiful hand-knit poncho, spoke on and on until, at last, he presented the Ordinary One with a key to the town and two ten-day old, baby black lambkins.

The lambs were so cute, until they peed on Ordinary Bob's black wool sweater with its gorgeous Navaho design. I'm sure this knit was available through the *Sundance* catalog. Ordinary Bob, compelled to feign surprise and delight, immediately unloaded these little bundles of joy back onto the Mayor, thankfully preventing his honor from saying more.

I never saw the little lambs again.

Bahhhhh.

Georgia O'Keeffe's house was certainly an eclectic and interesting location for the post screening party. But it wasn't very big. Mr. & Mrs. Got Rocks in Oil were so pleased to host the party they actually paid for the event.

Well, you get what you pay for. Regrettably, two hundred guests were crammed into a space that wasn't meant to hold thirty. It was the first week in April and southwestern nights in early spring are notoriously freezing. Every guest arrived bundled up, stepping from the twenty-five degrees outside into ninety degrees inside. They barely had enough space to take their coats off. The home was filled with incredible antiques that effectively blocked most foot traffic.

In this sea of sweltering humanity was placed a large hand-carved mission refectory table smothered by a sumptuous hors d'oeuvre buffet. The focal point of this gastronomic display was a huge silver platter piled lavishly high with bite-sized grilled baby lamp chops. Ravenous appetites diminished in horror.

Baahhhh!

To underscore this unfortunate choice of faire, Miss Assistant, the one smitten with Ol' Bob, invited him and his entourage for a midnight rendezvous to the barn. Tripping over wheat and oats, we had the fortunate opportunity to witness the birth of four baby lambs. It was very sweet to watch the mama welcome each new baby. Nothing compares to the "milagro" of birth, except, in this case, perhaps the expectation of a long and happy life.

Baahhh!

Chapter Nine

THE LAST TEMPTATION OF CHRIST

My likeness was crucified and stabbed in effigy on the studio's front lawn. My life was constantly threatened. I was forced to sneak into buildings through the back door, just so I wouldn't be the next victim of a hate crime.

As the head of publicity at Universal Studios, I became closely associated with each film released—the good, the bad and the ugly. When Universal announced it was making *The Last Temptation of Christ,* all hell broke loose with fundamental Christians. Universal prudently hired round-the-clock bodyguards for my protection. This period would be the most frightening, and emotionally unnerving of my illustrious career. Looking back on it, it was also one of the most interesting.

There are a lot of Christian fundamentalists who adhere to a very narrow interpretation of the Bible. The film did not. The Chairman never dreamed how deep these zealous feelings would go. Soon Universal and its parent company MCA was neck deep in a religious quagmire. As the studio spokesperson, I was hurled along with them, head first into this nightmare.

Director Martin Scorsese had long wanted to make a movie version of the Nikos Kazantzakis novel, *The Last Temptation of Christ.* He convinced Universal to take on the project. This was a controversial fictional "what if" story about the life of Jesus. It was considered a serious thought-provoking work and widely discussed in seminaries throughout the Christian world for many years.

In the book, Jesus is portrayed as a man who experiences every form of human temptation: fear, doubt, depression, and lust. As he is dying on the cross, he dreams he has married, sired children and has, in human terms, lived a normal life. As his dream fades, Jesus having finally over-come all human temptations, dies exclaiming, "It is accomplished."

To put it mildly, Marty's cast was unique. Willem Dafoe was a less than charismatic Jesus. Harvey Keitel portrayed a Judas with a New York accent. Barbara Hershey was a collagen-lipped Mary Magdalene, with her feet hennaed and bejeweled. Rock star David Bowie turned in an astonishing performance as Pontius Pilate, which I considered Oscar worthy. To keep costs down, the film was shot in the Moroccan desert.

Marty promised if Universal green lighted this picture (a movie no other studio was willing to make) that he'd shoot it in just fifty-eight days and bring it in for a budget of $7M. This little low-budget picture would wind up costing MCA millions more and thousands of man hours to undo the damage to their reputation.

My boss Ed Roginski had, at one time, entered the seminary to become a priest. He understood from the beginning that the studio would be inviting controversy, and fought mightily against this project. "Leave it alone," he cautioned. Any substantive discussion about religion and God tends to become a volatile minefield.

The Chairman, who was still new on the studio scene, desperately wanted to form an alliance with Scorsese. Especially since Marty's films like *Goodfellas* made mega bucks. He thought that *The Last Temptation of Christ* was a good way to open the door to securing a deal for Marty's next big blockbuster. So he flat out ignored Ed's warnings.

The Christian Right began screaming, "Universal's Jews crucify Jesus again!" Although I am a gentile, I was placed directly in their crosshairs. It was time to embrace a crisis management position. I immediately did and wasted no time securing a select group of outside advisors to help us.

The advice we got was not to go head-to-head with anyone based on religious doctrine. This would be ineffectual. However, it was best to address the overwhelming backlash from the standpoint of free speech. In this country any person or group has the right to express their thoughts or concepts on any subject. Whether someone chooses to boycott the film or view it was beside the point. Universal had a moral obligation to protect this picture's right-of-release under the First Amendment.

Much feuding went on between the Catholic Church, the Fundamentalist Right, the Jewish Defense League, the Aryan Nation, and many others. I was part of a huge developing news story and ensnared in the middle of history being made. No one needs to be that famous, or should I say infamous.

Many journalists and authors have written extensively about the serious aspects of *The Last Temptation of Christ*. A book released in 2009 entitled, *The Siege of Hollywood,* by Thomas Lindlof, details at great length the making and marketing of the picture. If you are interested in what transpired, it would be a good book to read.

Through the years I have discovered that humor can be found in even the most dire of situations. *The Last Temptation of Christ* (LTOC) was no exception.

Towards the end of this chapter you will be introduced to two individuals I fondly call, "Moron Number One" (M1) and "Moron Number Two" (M2). M1 and M2 were charged with overseeing the protection of the Universal Studio lot. Unfortunately they were bumbling idiots. Thankfully, they had a lot of help from real professionals. Their names are "changed" to offer them the protection they haphazardly secured for others.

Universal's security was not insignificant. There was a heavily manned guard gate at every entrance. Incoming mail was routinely inspected by the Universal City Post Office. And there were usually more armed bodyguards floating around than there were actors to protect. All guests visiting buildings on the lot were subjected to gate and lobby identification checks.

With all the security in place, M1 and M2 had never come close to dealing with a real protection crisis. So when one finally happened, they went straight into a "Laurel and Hardy" act I wished I had filmed.

The LTOC media crisis heated up by the hour. I received dozens of death threats a day via phone calls and mail. A local nut case named Bible Billy staged an impromptu prayer session in front of MCA Chairman Lew Wasserman's house and dumped pig's blood all over his driveway. This infuriated Lew's outspoken wife Edie. It was at this point that M1 and M2 decided Mr. Wasserman and I needed full-time protection.

If you are thinking a Kevin Costner type of bodyguard, then think again.

I was assigned three teams of two guards each who worked eight-hour shifts. My daytime guys were two retired cops probably in their early sixties. One's claim to fame was that he happened to be the cop who pulled mass murderer Charles Manson by the hair out of his hiding place under a building at the Manson cult compound.

The second duo varied each afternoon, but each team was comprised of off-duty Los Angeles Department Asian task force cops. These guys were tough. They told the best stories too. I'd cook dinner, and they'd entertain me. For instance, did you know that the way street hookers avoid being arrested by undercover cops is to tell the supposed John who pulls up curbside to, "zip it down and pull it out" before they will get into the car? Cops are strictly forbidden to do any unzipping, since that's considered entrapment. So if the guy refuses to wink his weenie, the prostitute figures it's a set-up. I learned a lot of things from these gentlemen that I have tucked away in case I ever write a cop drama.

I never saw my overnight guys. They just snuck around my apartment at night while I slept and were gone by morning. I always left them snacks like you would for Santa; donuts and coffee left by the fireplace. Their present to me was that I was still breathing each morning. Not a bad gift.

It sounds glamorous to have bodyguards. But it isn't fun at all when you see them look under your car for bombs or you try to shop for new bras and they're right there with you. If I headed down the hall from my office to go to the bathroom one followed. If I went to a friend's house for dinner, one sat in front of the house and the other in back. You could forget about romantic dates. I endured six months of this 24/7 protection.

Another major precaution was that "Sally Van Slyke" ceased to exist on all public records. I was deleted from any property references. My driver's license and passport were marked unlisted. Every published record that could be used to locate me was expunged. It was a mini version of what they do to those in the witness protection program.

One Sunday night about two weeks into my guardianship, I received a call around eleven. It was the Universal main guard gate asking if I was with my guards and was I all right? "Yes to both," I answered. "Why?"

What they said next frightened me so much that I felt a sudden chill and began to shake.

The main gate had been quiet Sunday evening. Few cars came or went. There was no foot traffic. Suddenly a glowing red flash went off on the front lawn some fifty feet or so away just out of view. One guard immediately ran over to check it out and discovered two lifelike dolls propped on the lawn. The first, a male doll resembling Lew Wasserman, had been crucified on a cross. The attached sign read, "This Jew Killed Jesus."

The second doll was a redheaded female attached to a board with her legs spread eagle, a knife coming out of her vagina dripping real blood. A cardboard sign read, "This is what will happen to Sally Van Slyke."

Whoa. Wait a minute here.

Not to worry? Enter now M1 and M2. Rushing to the scene, M1 and M2 were handling the dolls, poking lifting and moving them. It was only after they had trampled all over the crime scene that they called the real police. Why not just toss the dolls back and forth, or better yet, put them in chairs and have a tea party? "This is another fine mess you've gotten us into Ollie!"

I went ballistic. I couldn't sleep a wink the rest of the night. By the next morning I was an exhausted, half-crazed woman. When I finally talked to M1 and M2, I ripped them a new one! No shit. I came unglued at their stupidity and started peeling the paint off the walls, I was so livid. To their credit, they just stood there and took it as I belittled them.

Next I marched upstairs to check on Lew Wasserman.

"You scared?" he asked.

"Hell yes, I am," I answered. "Do you think they're going to kill us?"

"Maybe. But I doubt it," he replied somewhat ingeniously. "They don't have the balls. They're just trying to scare you."

"Well, I'm exhausted and fed up." I hated to admit it but I was scared. I asked him, "What about you? Are you scared?"

"Well, Mrs. W is not very happy," he chortled. Edie Wasserman was an outspoken person with a temper. She could speak her mind.

Lew went on, "Sally, you never should have been put in this position. I'm sorry, and I'm prepared to do whatever you want me to do to get you out of this."

This of course meant he was willing to offer me a big payoff to bail out. This was my chance to negotiate a lucrative golden exit deal, but like an idiot I asked, "What would you do?"

Give Lew Wasserman a chance to schmooze, and he'd do it with such grace and elegance you'd end up buying swampland from him for more than the asking price. He shared this skill with his old friend President Lyndon Baines Johnson who was a master of the art.

"I'd stick around. They aren't going to kill us. Let's tough this one out and go down in history together holding hands. Remember, all things pass. Think about it, and let me know your decision tomorrow."

With that I left and went back to my office.

Lew knew I wasn't going anywhere. The terrorists had scared me, but mostly they had succeeded in pissing me off. If they wanted a fight, I'd give them one. Besides, the idea of heading into the history books holding hands with Lew Wasserman appealed to me. I had always respected him but was now really becoming fond of this icon.

The fact that I had not yet even seen the film made my situation more difficult. Did I mention that the outcry over this film was *prior* to the film being released? Marty had been dragging his feet and the picture was still in editing. He had been apprehensive to show the picture to anyone at the studio. This is what I continually told the press all throughout the protests. I know this is Scorsese I'm talking about, but enough already! I had to get a look at this picture, NOW! So I flew to New York to be the first executive to screen the movie. Marty's office was located in the famous Brill Building on Broadway and 47th but the screening was held very quietly in a rented theater a few blocks away. I'd flown in on the red eye and had to stay awake until 2 pm when the screening began.

The film ran 164 minutes, just short of three hours. However, given my lack of sleep and state-of-mind, it felt much, much longer. After the credits rolled, I was surprised to admit that I saw nothing blasphemous about it. However, I also didn't find anything very compelling about it.

Willem Dafoe is a competent yet unexciting low energy actor. He simply did not have the personal presence to portray Jesus (if you believe as I do, that Jesus must have been a very charismatic man). Harvey Keitel's accent was an interesting choice for Judas but out of

Sally and Lew Wasserman. You can see three
of their bodyguards in the background.

kilter somehow. Barbara Hershey pouted away and just looked whor-
ish. David Bowie, however, played his five-minute cameo as the sneering
Pontius Pilate with such elegant detachment that his performance really
jumped off the screen. Simply outstanding.

I promised The Chairman I'd call in my report immediately following the screening. He picked up the phone with great anticipation. "Is it
brilliant?" he asked.

I chose my words carefully. "It is very artistic," I replied evenly.

"What does that mean?" he sounded disappointed.

"It is artistically interesting," I repeated. "So we can get away with calling it an artistic masterpiece, and the critics will probably embrace that. As to how *brilliant* it is, you decide that for yourself."

What I didn't say to The Chairman that day was in fact uttered a month or so down the road by California's former and now current governor, Jerry Brown. He attended an early private viewing of the picture and bluntly stated, "It's dull. Dafoe doesn't have any charisma. The best thing you have going for this picture is the controversy."

Amen to that. Jerry's assessment was spot on. The controversy turned out to be great for generating interest in the film. However, for MCA, the negative reaction resulted in a Judas kiss of death. LTOC was a picture that never should have been made by a major studio with stock investors.

The Christian Right called for a strict boycott against all MCA-owned companies which included The Universal Studio's tour, Spencer Gifts, and even...Yosemite National Park. A massive demonstration against the film was staged in early July on Lankershim Boulevard directly in front of the studio's main gate. Pat Robertson, Jerry Falwell, and other prominent Christian leaders led the massive demonstration that included a natty little group on Harley motorcycles proudly displaying flyers that read *Bikers For Jesus.* Dozens of news helicopters flew overhead, ground camera crews jockeyed for position. Universal phone lines were jammed. The nightly network news broadcasts led with the story. Picketers appeared everywhere.

At this point we knew it was vital (sooner rather than later) to show the picture to religious leaders of all denominations. We immediately set up a secret screening to be held in Manhattan. We asked our invitees not to notify the press and as a safety precaution to meet at a central west side hotel location for lunch prior to the showing. After eating, they would board a bus and be driven to the location for the screening. Some of the guests included former Catholic Priest Daniel Berrigan, the Catholic Film Review Board, the Senior Bishop of the Episcopal Church, and several First Amendment Rights organizations. I also included an acquaintance of mine, former Catholic Father Terry Sweeney who was, in fact, married in real life. In the film Jesus fantasizes about having a marriage and living a normal life. I was especially anxious to hear Terry's reaction.

I was raised an Episcopalian. When my Bishop Paul Moore of

St. John the Divine in NYC arrived for the lunch I heaved a sigh of relief. "Bishop Moore," I began. "I am in such trouble with my mother. She thinks this whole thing is in poor taste. To her, it's worse than if I committed armed robbery! What do I tell her?"

"Well, Sally dear," he began, "tell her she is right. It is in poor taste, but it is fascinating nonetheless. Ask her if she doesn't agree with that assessment."

I was doomed.

Thankfully I didn't have much time to think about my fate, because we apparently had a leak. The picketers and press were out front clamoring at the door. Some guests walked in unnoticed as they were wearing ordinary street garb, but others wearing a frock or vestments went through chaos getting in. Picketers yelled all kinds of slurs and threats at them.

As lunch was served I headed for the theater. I'd been there for the sound check earlier that morning and had run into Paul Newman. I mean literally smacked right into him. We were both looking for Marty who hadn't arrived yet. Paul was going to watch the sound check. While we waited for Marty to show, we sat side by side in the theater and I read out loud the latest article about the crisis from that morning's *New York Times*. Stressed and tired as I was, I wasn't so far gone that it didn't register with me that, "Oh my gosh I'm reading to Paul Newman."

Now if he'd played Jesus we would have been somewhere. Paul had charisma up the ying yang. And those blue eyes. Unbelievable. I cheered up.

Following lunch, the guests were loaded on buses and headed for the *23rd Street Cineplex Odeon* on the Lower West Side. Hoards of press and picketers followed us bumper to bumper.

There were perhaps fifty in attendance including our Chairman. I elected not to sit through another screening of the picture, opting instead to perch nervously outside the theater eating my replacement lunch, popcorn. Two hours plus went slowly by. I was zoning out. Suddenly the lights flickered off and then back on in the entire complex. I jumped up in alarm spilling my popcorn all over the lobby and ran to the theater door just in time to meet The Chairman as he slammed out screaming.

"We were just in the middle of the crucifixion and suddenly the film stopped and everything plunged into darkness. There aren't any lights in there!"

One of my staffers grabbed The Chairman and quickly locked him in the manager's office, guarding the door. I, in turn, screamed for security, becoming intensely aware of my surroundings.

Finally we located the security personnel that was supposed to be on duty. You guessed it, M1 and M2. They were across the street in the park enjoying the sunny weather, not a care in the world.

"What? What?" they yelled in unison, tripping over each other as they raced back to the theater. Well, it took them five minutes, but that was racing for them.

In the meantime, someone had gone to look for the projectionist and finally located him in a bathroom stall upstairs. He claimed he had just left the booth for a minute to go to the bathroom and simply had no idea what was transpiring. I pointed out to him it had been a damn long minute.

Then M1 and M2 chimed in, "We did see someone try to enter the side door a few minutes ago, but didn't think anything of it since we had checked earlier and that door was locked." Did it occur to these guys that someone might have unlocked it? Duh.

"Didn't that give you a clue something might be up?" I asked.

They answered with surprise, "You mean you think someone did this on purpose?"

"Geez, you think fellas?" I said disgusted. "Exactly what are the odds that the film stops just on the crucifixion before Jesus has his dream?"

"Gosh, Sally, when you put it that way. Maybe somebody's guilty of sabotage?"

Damn they were quick.

The Chairman remained locked safely in the manager's office while I went in to speak with the audience. "I apologize to you all," I began earnestly, "We seem to have experienced some technical difficulty but I am assured the film will continue within five minutes. Thank you for your patience."

"It's okay Sally. This is where the story ends for most of us anyway." It was the infamous Daniel Berrigan who decided to speak for his colleagues present. This former Jesuit priest was an outspoken protestor of the Vietnam War, appearing on the 1960's FBI's ten most wanted list, and served many years in prison for perceived illegal activities.

We did get the film back up and running. When the screening finally ended, I shook everyone's hand and thanked them for "walking the plank" to attend. I would see some later that evening at a dinner we'd planned at the Regency Hotel for a select few to do the meet-and-greet with Marty. I arranged this one-on-one so some key attendees could ask the director questions. The Catholic Review Board representatives were an important part of the meet-and-greet. How they ruled on this picture would make a crucial difference to the film's reception.

Naturally I would act as the hostess for the dinner as well. We had reserved a private dining room just off the lobby at the Regency. The oblong table seated twenty. I sat at one end and The Chairman at the other. Marty sat in the middle so that everyone could hear him. Ironically, the whole scene reminded me of The Last Supper. Bishop Moore sat on Marty's right and the head of the Catholic Review Board on his left.

Three fully-vetted servers (according to M1 and M2) attended to our service for the evening. Guests were offered a simple choice between grilled salmon or medallions of filet mignon. A great deal of wine was poured.

I had placed Father Terry Sweeney on my left. I knew this man going back to my Metromedia publicist days when I had worked with then Jesuit Father Sweeney on a documentary he directed while at Loyola University. It was entitled *Streets of Anger, Streets of Hope* and he received an Emmy Award for his efforts.

Terry had once served as the religious consultant for the highly acclaimed television mini-series, *The Thorn Birds*. I always felt that he was too appealing to women to stay single for long. I knew it was only a matter of time before he was defrocked. I was right. He met his wife while serving communion. As she recalls it, "I received communion, the blood of Christ, from him. Looking up into his eyes, I took my sip of wine and knew he was the only man for me." Terry was suspended from the Jesuits, and I am not sure if he had been excommunicated as well. He appeared at our dinner in his full clerical garb. He still had make-up on left over from a local television interview that afternoon. What a fascinating dinner conversation we had.

Our fully-vetted servers were doing very nicely. What was rather strange, however, was that the door to the dining room would open every so often and a ghost like character, straight out of a Tim Burton film, would amble in one door and out another. The closest modern day example I can think of would be a performer from Cirque de Soleil with white face paint, huge eyes, and colorful garb. One ethereal gentleman walked through on stilts wearing a rainbow morning coat, balloon clown pants, and black top hat. A three-hundred-pound woman waddled through in a Swan Lake outfit. That's all they did. In one door and out the other. Those of us facing the door all did our best to ignore this bazar caravan but hey....it eerily occurred to me...where were M1 and M2? Who were these oddities anyway?

I excused myself to look for The Hardy Boys. "Morons where are yoooou?"

Just as I suspected, they were in the bar protecting the alcohol.

"That's weird," they both replied as I told them what was happening. Ya think, fellas? How's about you check it out? Later they claimed they didn't see anyone fitting that description hanging around.

When the dinner ended I had the distinct feeling that the Catholic Review Board was going to rule against seeing this film, which ultimately they did. Meanwhile, all I wanted to do was go to my room, slip into my jammies and sleep. My parting comment to The Chairman and his wife was that my parents would be really ticked if I was offed after they worked so hard to raise me.

Back in my hotel room I decided I was too wound up to sleep. I also discovered I forgot to bring my nightgown, so I slipped on one of our tie-in promotional T-shirts from a picture called *Midnight Run*. I decided to pour myself a nice glass of the hotel's gift swill and click on *Letterman* for a quick laugh or two. Seated comfortably on the sitting room sofa, I hit the remote control On button. Suddenly the television sparked, smoked, and then exploded with a boom!

Yowza! Feet don't fail me now. Flinging my wine glass across the room, I raced out the door into the hallway.

"Help!"

Just then the elevator doors slid open and I came face to face with about a dozen semi-blitzed conventioneers who just stared at me. That was when I realized I was merely wearing a rather short T-shirt, which boldly read, "I'm on the Midnight Run for Charity."

"Which charity?" one leisure suit asked.

"I'll support them," another slobbered.

I tugged on the hem of the shirt in front of me attempting to cover up. I then turned around, which was worse, so I quickly turned back, deciding instead to go on the offensive and just stare them down. Finally, the automatic doors closed and I heard them all scream with laughter as they headed up.

Wouldn't you know it. My suite door had self-locked when I ran from the room. There I stood in the hallway with no phone. Unless I really wanted to create a stir, I had no way to get to the lobby for another key. Looking around in a panic, I discovered there was no house phone either. There was essentially nothing I could do except slink into the emergency exit staircase and hide. About a half-hour later a maid came along and was startled to see a half-naked woman trying her hardest to look inconspicuous. English was not her language of choice and it took my best pantomiming to communicate my difficulties. She obviously was finding my story suspicious and called security. When the house dick showed up, M1 and M2 were in tow. I was finally ushered back into the comfort and relative safety of my suite.

I had to wait a full hour before the hotel engineer, summoned by M1, showed up to determine why the TV blew up. The engineer was flummoxed. M1 and M2 decided it must have been a loose connection. I wasn't going to argue.

After all, those boys specialized in loose connections.

Chapter Ten

ARNOLD AND DANNY: THE UNLIKELIEST OF TWINS

Bam! Arnold slammed the phone down on me again.
What an asshole, I thought. Can you imagine if
Arnold Schwarzenegger ever had any real power?
Could you see him as an elected official?

Arnold Schwarzenegger and Danny DeVito were *Twins.* At least they were in the soon to be released potential holiday blockbuster movie, *Twins.* A Presidential Premiere was planned for the Kennedy Center benefiting Special Olympics, the organization headed by Arnold's mother-in-law Eunice Shriver. I was delighted to have a potential hit on my hands and, at the same time, have the opportunity to work for such a great cause and organize it in tandem with such a fabulous woman.

Naturally, Universal would pick up the tab for everything. And "everything" turned out to be a State Department luncheon, a VIP cocktail reception, followed by a screening at the Kennedy Center, and capped off with a huge dinner dance at the Shriver's Potomac, Maryland estate. Slated for the last week in November, the party would require a tent the size of Texas to be erected on the Shriver's back lawn. Heating this enormous structure alone would cost thousands. Several times a month I traveled back and forth to Washington for meetings with caterers, State Department coordinators and holiday tree trimmers. Soon my budget, if there ever was one, flew out the window and sailed away.

At our first meeting, Mrs. Shriver insisted I call her Eunice. I confess I found it difficult. I grew up in the Kennedy era and had a genuine reverence for JFK. It seemed somehow disrespectful to call his sister, the founder of Special Olympics, by her first name. However, eventually I overcame my shyness because Eunice was extremely candid and accessible. She could fight with you one minute and play tennis with you the

77

next. She was a skillful politician in her own right.

Washington, D.C. is the toughest town in the U.S. in which to stage events. During a national election, it is a task beyond all reason. Attention is limited and feathers easily ruffled on both sides of the aisle. Even an insignificant film premiere becomes political. Coordinating the seating plan alone for the State Department luncheon became a nightmare of epic proportions. Eunice had retained a local public relations firm to fill in the organizational gaps, but they did not do a damn thing! In fact, they ducked every task handed to them. So in the end, the political and social faux pas that are inevitable in any big event would be mine to claim.

Washington is all about seating. Where you're seated tells the world how important you are. Was former Secretary of Defense Robert McNamara more important than *Washington Post* owner Katherine Graham? Was Evangeline Bruce, wife of the former Ambassador to the Court of St. James, more celebrated than Washington's Grande Dame, Buffy Cafritz? Calling the situation a nightmare was an understatement.

I agonized over it. Fortunately Eunice, who was no stranger to Washington politics, took it all in stride. Eunice consulted with her daughter Maria (Arnold's wife), who she deferred to often, and they changed a few people around. She sat me between McNamara and Evangeline Bruce. I was honored, very touched, and looked forward to a delightful lunch.

As the seating began, Marylouise Oates, former *Los Angeles Times* Gossip columnist, immediately cornered me. "Oatsie," as she was nicknamed, had recently married Bob Shrum, a very successful campaign speechwriter and adviser to many top democrats. Oatsie, a good friend of Lew Wasserman, the CEO of Music Corporation of America (MCA), was deeply upset with her seat. MCA is Universal's parent company, and Lew Wasserman my ultimate boss. Oatsie suggested I trade my seat with hers.

Hindsight being twenty-twenty, I realize now I should have told Oatsie to take a hike. Regrettably, and in the interest of diplomacy, I made the switch. My seat partners for the afternoon turned out to be Senator Edward Kennedy and a former network United Nations reporter who (she made it way too obvious) was hot for Teddy. The luncheon moved on, and an abundance of wine was poured. Teddy wasn't feeling much pain so all went swimmingly, if somewhat incoherently.

Security at the Kennedy Center that night was tight as a drum. President-elect George Bush (senior) and family would be attending. Although I was issued the Secret Service (SS) top security clearance for the evening, I still had to pass through two metal detectors to enter the inner sanctum and another to go to the ladies room. (Not sure what they expected me to sneak into the ladies room. I wasn't wearing a wire or an under-wire for that matter.)

The plan was that a VIP reception for two hundred of the biggest contributing guests would be in full swing in the reception hall adjacent to the main theater when President-elect Bush arrived. The remaining hundreds of lesser contributors would be seated immediately upon arrival at the Center. The plan, approved in advance with the SS, was that Bush and family would simply walk through the VIP reception, nodding to all, and then move on to the backstage area. Once the VIP guests were ushered to their screening seats, Sargent Shriver would step out and introduce the President-elect to ALL the guests. The President-elect would make a short speech about the value of Special Olympics (lovely remarks for which I had written the text). He would then be joined on stage by our stars and the all-important photo opportunity would take place; million-dollar faces all smiling to polite applause. Sounds straightforward, right?

Wrong.

An ebullient Sargent Shriver became confused, grabbed Bush during the VIP walk-through and proceeded to introduce him to the much smaller crowd. Bush became equally confused and delivered his scripted remarks to this much smaller group with no press coverage and no cameras clicking. Meanwhile, the seated main audience was patiently awaiting his now late arrival.

You know something is seriously amiss when SS agents begin whispering into their cuffs. They headed straight for me. You don't fool with Mother Nature, and you don't make changes to a President's schedule without clearing it first with the SS.

"Hey fellas," I squeaked. "I'm as confused as you are."

These guys weren't happy. They immediately herded the Bushes backstage. I followed and quickly began composing a different speech for the President to deliver—to the entire assembly this time. In light of our new timing issues the all-important photo op would now happen back-stage. Thankfully, I would still capture the photo that all America would see on front pages tomorrow morning.

Herding cats must be easier than getting these fat cats to gather all in one place and on cue. The first to bail on this photo op was, ironically, the first lady-elect, Barbara Bush. Instead of following our directions, she grabbed a bag of greasy buttered popcorn and headed up to the Presidential box with sons George W. and Jeb dutifully in tow to await opening credits.

Danny DeVito, the diehard Democrat, wanted to opt out as well. "No way," I hissed at him, grabbing his almost five-foot frame and dragging him upfront, "Get in that shot now!" With most of my "cats" in place, the camera began clicking away. Suddenly Danny lifted up his arm and made donkey ears behind the President-elect's head. Then he stuck his tongue out at the unsuspecting future leader of the free world. I glared at him menacingly, but what could I say? Smiling sweetly, I went over and bopped Danny on his head. Later I reminded the official photographer that any photograph with donkey ears or a tongue out was never to see the light. Capische?

Finally everyone settled down to watch the picture. If laughter meant success, then we certainly were going to have one. Yeah! The Washington elite loved the movie.

Miracle of miracles, the *Farmer's Almanac* got the forecast right for the night, or partly so. It did not snow in Washington. Instead it poured —by the bucketful! The usual half-hour drive to the Shriver house took twice as long as we navigated through blustery torrents. Riding in the lead car, I looked back and all I could make out were miles of blurred headlights through the rear windshield wipers swishing at top speed. The SS put the kibosh on the Bush's attending, so the entire Bush family was transplanted to the Blair House and their nice warm beds. Damn! How lucky can you get?

The Shrivers' traditional two-story, white clapboard house was a welcoming sight. Guests entered through a large entrance hall flanked by giant portraits of President JFK and his older brother Joseph, who died while on a flying mission in WWII. In the soft evening light these portraits appeared especially poignant, as if the brothers were gazing fondly at each other.

The rooms off the hallway were blocked to nosey guests by stanchions. Glancing beyond the velvet ropes one could view a magnificent mahogany dining room table, elegantly set for twenty. Six or seven attractively dressed young men and women were chatting comfortably in the main living room and adjacent library. Quite frankly, these were the best-looking security guards I've ever seen.

Passing through the French doors into the enormous tent, guests were treated to a beautifully decorated and well-heated space completely decked out for the holidays with a half dozen fifteen-foot lighted fir trees. At center stage, a very hip dance band played contemporary versions of all the holiday classics. Five fully-stocked service bars were doing a booming business. Four double-sided dinner buffets stood at the ready. There was round formal seating for all surrounding a dance floor that waited for the merry making to begin. A royal red carpet replaced the standard Astroturf flooring, and multi-tiered gold candelabra highlighted the center of each buffet. Our months of meticulous planning could be seen in the details. In spite of how hard I'd tried to reign in the budget, we hadn't skimped on a thing.

Wonder Woman Lynda Carter was holding court at the entrance and pulled me aside to let me know she suspected the food might get cold. Why tell me? Did she have a premonition I'd become a caterer someday? Now that's a wonder woman!

Senator Kennedy hovered at the bar closest to the door with his date, who might have been a lovely person but she looked like a hooker and so the "buzzing" began. Appearing uncomfortable, the Senator was apologizing to all (who couldn't have cared less) for missing the screening. Barbara Walters with current fling, Senator John Warner, appeared to be in a deep conversation with Eunice, when Eunice suddenly bowed out and began chasing after her daughter who was careening around perched on four-inch stilettos, wearing a dress that resembled a tutu, and sporting an unusually teased hairdo. Maria puffed on her cigarette while looking for Arnold who had just disappeared with Danny.

This was turning out to be a typical Washington event, the definition for which is everyone running around after everyone else trying desperately to be seen in the "right" scene.

President Kennedy's sisters, Patricia and Jean, were shadowing Donald Trump. Donald Trump was in turn dogging me. When I finally let him catch up with me, The Donald demanded to know, "Why do the people at MCA hate me so much?"

"Why ever not?" I replied and slunk away.

I left the party at midnight utterly exhausted. The dancing was still going full tilt. Didn't many of these notable red faces have to get up early tomorrow morning to attend to our nation's sensitive business on C-Span? Frightening.

And speaking of sensitive work, the next morning Arnold and Danny were set to fly to Chicago for an appearance on Oprah. It was Sweeps month, when ratings count most to networks and advertisers. So ABC had been touting "Mutt and Jeff's" appearance on the show for over two weeks.

The boys were set to fly from Dulles to O'Hare at ten o'clock in the morning on United. Why not a private plane like every other major movie star? Because I had strict instructions from my Chairman that, under no circumstances, was I to hire a private plane for Arnold. It seemed that Arnold had bested my fearless leader negotiating one of the savviest Hollywood contracts ever heard of. Arnold had been given a piece of the action off the top and was set to make mega-millions from the deal. This insult to the Chairman's ego of course resulted in the inevitable "whose dick is bigger," and "boyz will be boyz" game.

Three guesses whose was and the first two don't count!

It was just after seven in the morning when the phone woke me out of a sound, blissful sleep. I suspected there would be trouble and was afraid that this might be it. It was Arnold.

"Good morning," Arnold began. "Where's my private plane parked?"

"Good morning to you," I croaked. "You're set to fly commercial this morning with Danny—remember?"

Arnold paused for a moment and then retorted, "I'm not flying commercial into O'Hare. It's a dangerous airport. I want a private plane or I'm not going."

Was he serious? I tried to keep it friendly, "Arnold, don't be silly. Millions of people fly into O'Hare every week."

"I don't give a damn what millions of ordinary people do," he screamed!

Oh-oh. He was getting mad and loud. I had to pull the receiver away from my ear. But I had one more card to play. "Arnold, may I remind you that Oprah was in your wedding? For God's sake, you can't leave her hanging out to dry. You simply have to show up!"

"I'm not going without a private plane, and I'm not the one hanging anyone out," he snarked. "You are!"

Slam!

Asshole!

Still, this was no time to whimper. I had to try to coerce Mr. Pump-You-Up to Chicago and into Oprah's waiting arms. So I called my Chairman's room to beg for mercy. However, not being a fool, he'd already hopped on a commercial flight and was on his way to LA by now, sipping a mimosa. I knew that no other underling was going to get involved in this one. I was on my own, again.

I called Danny, who frankly couldn't care less what he flies on. "Pleeeese...call Arnold....talk some sense into him."

"Yeah yeah...okay. Wish me luck," he croaked out.

I loved Danny. Unfortunately, he was back on the horn within two minutes.

"He ain't gonna go. So I guess I ain't gonna go either. See you back in L.A." Danny hung up the phone.

Nothing to do but call Oprah's producer, listen to the tirade and head home myself. Fortunately, I was in possession of a first-class ticket on United's eleven AM direct flight from Dulles into LAX. I was holding it just in case I had to skip Chicago and fly back to the LA studio to handle some unexpected catastrophe. Well, I had one now. There was nothing left to do but drag my beleaguered carcass to Dulles, get on board, strap myself in and request a stiff double before take-off.

I arrived at Dulles. A perk of my position was that I always flew first class. Normally I would have been met at the curb and escorted by a Hoffman VIP travel rep. However, time had been short this morning, so I did not check in at the main concourse but proceeded directly to the gate via shuttle. My confirmed ticket with a seat assignment moved me straight through security.

"I'm Sally Van Slyke," I said leaning over the counter adjacent to the entry gate for my flight that was currently boarding. Without a word, the ticket lady handed me my boarding pass which I noticed was for coach. I politely called her attention to the obvious error. She ever so sweetly corrected MY unfortunate misunderstanding.

"No, you're flying coach today Miss Von Shike," she said without looking up.

"No," I replied cordially. "My ticket clearly indicates first class, seat B2." I pushed the ticket back toward her.

She took the ticket from me and said, "I understand your confusion Miss Van Silkie but you did not confirm in time so you are flying coach today. You were never completely booked on first class, and first class is completely full on this flight."

Getting increasingly annoyed, I motioned to her and the ticket, "Have you looked at the ticket I just handed you?"

"Yes I have madame and there appears to have been some mistake with it. I assure you, the airline has you booked on coach." Then she harrumphed!

Before I could harrumph back, the door to the VIP lounge opened and guess who strode out? The Terminator himself prowled past, spotted me and flipped me the "Hasta la vista, baby" scowl. Then I noticed Danny peeking out from behind him and waiving to me. Maria followed, struggling with her own carry-on.

I was not a happy camper. I turned again to "Miss Information" and said, "So I'm on coach? Just when did that trio book their seats? Did you know that I'm the one signing the payment vouchers for that trilogy of tickets?"

I did not stop there, but ragged on making it crystal clear to her that I didn't like being lied to. United Airlines would be well advised to have a senior representative meet me at the gate in L.A. if they wanted any of Universal's business in the future. Oh my God, I had just morphed into Arnold. I shut up and marched my bitch self onto the plane.

There he was. His big butt plopped into my B-2 surrounded by a handful of first-class startled and starry-eyed lobbyists. As I passed MY seat, I whacked Arnold with my carry-on and trekked the mile or so back to coach. We sat on the tarmac for what seemed hours, while the pilot explained they were just loading a few late pieces of luggage. Oh gee, who did those belong to?

Squeezed into coach I was ready to grab some shut-eye. I glanced up just in time to see Arnold thunking down the aisle towards me. What did the big boy want now? He leaned over the seat in front of me, staring me full in the face. "You'd better not tell Oprah this is my fault."

"Oh no?" I quipped. "Then exactly whose fault is it, Arnold?"

He leaned in even closer. "It's your fault. Because I fly on private planes for work, and you refused to give me one."

I had reached the breaking point and retorted, "You've known the rules of this game for a long time now Arnold. Why don't you just grow the hell up!"

Well, that pissed him off. Mr. Flex turned bright red as he went into the best Terminator impression of himself I've ever seen. Thrusting his ginormous face two inches from mine, he hissed, "If you blame me, you'll regret it!"

I yelped back, "Are you threatening me Arnold?" I must confess the thought of a little plastic surgery and half of what he was worth wouldn't be so bad. Come on, go for it—hit me!

Unfortunately I never got an answer. We were so fixated on our little drama that we'd both completely missed several announcements from the flight attendant requesting passengers take their seats. A flight attendant tapped Arnold on the shoulder. He spun around on her so quickly that she was startled and stepped back.

"Please take your seat Mr. Schwarzenegger." She was authoritative yet calm.

"You want ME to take my seat?" He was losing it.

This was getting out of hand. The man in the seat next to the one Arnold was leaning over took this as his cue to jump into the fray. "The lady told you to sit down man. So go sit down. I want to go home to my family."

The Terminator spun on him. Turning bright red he yelled, "You... are...telling...me...to...what..?

The man did not let Arnold finish. "I said sit the fuck down Mr. Schwarzenegger."

Ouch. Way to go!

Now here was a real live action hero. Fight. Fight. Fight. If I was a betting person, my money would have been on the new guy. I guess Arnold thought so, too, because without another word he stalked back down the aisle took my seat in first class and remained parked in it for the entire flight. I was relieved that he did not utter, "I'll be back."

Maria looked exhausted and nowhere near her usual coiffed self. She apparently did not have the time to comb out the rat-nest remains of her "do" from the night before. She was slogging back and forth from first class to my seat in coach, desperate to come up with some way to save the situation for her friend Oprah. At one point, she even offered to pay for the private plane out of her own pocket! But a private plane is not inexpensive and Maria didn't have the cash in her checking account. She couldn't borrow it from Arnold, so she asked me if I would loan it to her. How pathetic was this going to get?

Three hours ahead of us, The Chairman had finally landed at LAX. I caught up with him plane phone to car phone. Begging, pleading, and manipulating, I finally managed to get him to agree to split the cost of the private plane with Maria. Our new plan was to land at LAX, jump into limos, head to the Santa Monica Airport and take off in a private plane back to Chicago. The taping of Oprah would have to be delayed, but we'd get there just in time.

This could work. I went to tell Danny. Now Danny is an easygoing guy, but wife Rhea Perlman isn't so obliging. I could hear her yelling on the phone even over the hum of the engines, "You're not doing any such thing Danny! You didn't make this mess and you aren't going to fix it!" I have to confess that I admired her position. As it turned out, so did Danny.

This drama was officially over, and there would be no curtain call. No one was headed to Chicago.

As our plane landed, a fellow coach passenger leaned towards me and said, "Lady, I don't know who you are, but this was the best in-flight entertainment I've ever had."

Chapter Eleven

ROBERT REDFORD HATES MY GUTS

*My job at Universal did not discriminate between the
great Oscar caliber films and films that lacked movie magic.
It was my task to make each and every film appear desirable
to watch and Oscar-worthy.*

The film *Havana,* directed by Sydney Pollack, and starring
Ol' Ordinary Bob, lacked movie magic. Redford, beloved for his usually
streaked tussled main, had his hair slicked back which was very un-
becoming. He attempted to portray a roguish 1950s Miami gambler
headed to Havana to try his luck. He looked old, displayed absolutely no
chemistry with co-star Lena Olin, and seemed remote. Let's not mince
words—the film stunk.

Following the first screening for the executives we all bravely, but
unsuccessfully, tried to hide our disappointment in the picture. Unless I
misread his subtle hints (which I didn't) Ol' Bob knew it wasn't good. As
a result, I strongly suspected Ol' Bob was about to make life miserable for
the studio. Consequently, The Chairman was about to make life miserable
for me. That's how it works in Hollywood. Shit rolls downhill.

Super agent Mike Ovitz represented Redford. Ovitz was the head
of Creative Artists Agency (CAA), the largest elephant in Hollywood.
CAA handled most everyone of box office note in tinsel town. Mike Ovitz
wielded a huge stick. He intimidated the hell out of most people, not an
admirable trait but effective. Years later, his tactics came back to haunt
him. I always got along with Mike and admit I sort of liked him. So I didn't
jump on the Ovitz-bashing bandwagon.

Ovitz knew we were in trouble with this picture. He called a meeting
to discuss *Havana's* marketing plans. I was alarmed when the man himself
arrived at Universal's conference room for this lunchtime confab. Muhammad coming off the mountain indicated serious trouble was brewing.

Here's the skinny:

If everyone involved with the film knows it sucks and it doesn't have any legs, then it's an absolute *must* to open with a huge box office bang. This way, you get one good box office weekend before word-of-mouth lets out that the golden goose laid a rotten egg.

A biggie-bang-bang opening involves costly ads on television and in print, coveted covers of magazines, and a last-minute national press junket. Last-minute being the critical piece of the marketing puzzle. Limit the time journalists have to spread their "boo-boo" reviews. Put off for a few precious days the four thumbs down.

The Chairman knew Universal was about to eat it on this picture. Havana cost the studio a fortune to make, so he was unhinged and down-right frenzied. The task of making this scrambled mess palatable fell on me. He suggested, or should I say commanded, that I come up with some sort of press stunt involving Redford.

Ol' Ordinary Bob, on the other hand, was sending smoke signals from Utah that he had absolutely no intention of complying with any requests from Universal. I wasn't surprised. Ovitz wisely skated the middle, telling me he *hoped* he could convince Ol' Bob to agree to one or two limited press interviews. Ol' Bob's publicist, a chatty veteran by the name of Lois Smith, suddenly became impossible to reach by phone.

Every request was met with a "maybe."

The Chairman wanted the press junket as late as possible and not centered on the actual film. We needed to create an environment at this gathering that would make the film appear more compelling than it was. He suggested that perhaps we could make it more about Cuba and the chic high-rollers' mecca of the 50s in Havana. Perhaps we could even hold it in Cuba!

I reminded The Chairman that the picture had been shot in the Dominican Republic, because American citizens were barred from visiting Cuba. Landing in Cuba was not a viable option. However, we did come up with an alternative. Somewhat facetiously my staff and I put forth the idea of renting out an entire Carnival Cruise ship and inviting our national press for a weekend of sailing, recreation, gambling and frivolity while cruising *off the coast* of Cuba. Somewhere, tucked into the weekend of debauchery, the journalists would screen the film and subsequently interview the supporting cast led by director Sydney Pollack, who would be on board. Sunday afternoon we'd helicopter in Ol' Bob, land dramatically on the Lido deck, where he would step out, pose for a photo op and participate in a national televised interview or two.

I mean what the hell. If we were going to tank, let's throw more coin at the sinking ship. While we were at it, why not hand out contraband Cuban cigars? Ovitz surprisingly bought into this idea and agreed to run it past Ol' Bob.

The red phones went off all over town. Ol' Bob wasn't in for a helicopter ride. Idea overboard!

If at first you don't succeed—bail. Sorry, not the right Captain's spirit? Let's try again and think *outside the box* this time. Maybe we'd get lucky and Ol' Bob would say, "Wow! That's great kids."

We came up with a new idea I hoped Ol' Bob would like. We would produce a television documentary on the career of Robert Redford and get one of the networks to air it the weekend before *Havana* opened. ALL were onboard for this *Titanic* of an idea. Terrific, now I could stop worrying.

I went to see my old friend Brandon Tartikoff, President of NBC. Ovitz had given him the thumbs up so the meeting was just a formality. We already had a deal. Universal would make and deliver the half-hour docuBORE, and NBC would air it the Sunday prior to our Friday opening. This way NBC and Universal could both lose money.

"Please," Brandon pleaded. "Don't make it as dull as the great one actually is. Put some sexiness into it." Brandon is gone now. But wherever he is in this universe I want him to know I tried to make it sexy. I really did! Some things are futile before the attempt.

Redford agreed to be interviewed for the documentary on the condition that Sydney Pollack take part in the same interview. This wasn't so bad, because Sydney directed *Out of Africa*, which will forever remain an audience favorite and was a recognizable actor in his own right. He was great in *Tootsie.* Sydney had the knack of putting Ol' Bob at ease.

So this interview would take up ten or twelve of the twenty-six minutes. The remaining time would consist of a montage of old footage and interviews with co-stars and film clips; Meryl S, Jane F, and Barbra S. I wanted Paul Newman but he wasn't available.

Our docu-title was the only thing sexy about this endeavor. We called it, *"Robert Redford: The Man, The Myth and The Women.* Brandon liked it. Sidney thought it was great and The Chairman told me everyone thought it was good. So I operated under the assumption that the title had been cleared with all the players. Wrong! In my haste, I broke my own number one rule: never make assumptions!

It seems The Chairman, in touch with Ovitz on a daily basis, somehow neglected to clear our title with him. Ovitz, in turn, needed to get the green light from Ol' Bob. Unaware of this little breach in etiquette, I sailed right off with our title straight to the bible for television viewing, the weekly magazine *TV Guide.* On deadline for the week in question, they immediately went to print.

Ink hit the page just as a hurricane of bile hit my office door. Apparently, Redford had physically recoiled at the title's last three words "and The Women." He hated it! Either we paid to have *TV Guide* rip and reprint or he'd......!!!!!

Ovitz conveyed the disastrous news to us via a scathing phone call to The Chairman. Our weekly production/marketing meeting was interrupted with the message, "Pick up the damn phone!" Ovitz let us know, in no uncertain terms, that Universal had crossed his eight thousand pound gorilla, pain-in-the-ass super-client. Crossing Bob meant we had crossed HIM too. Not good. Mike wasn't holding back and his accusations were hitting the mark. I looked over at The Chairman, who had turned a sickly shade of pale green. When the phone call ended, I knew the next marker called in would be mine. I was becoming increasingly pissed at The Chairman! What the hell kind of liar's poker was he playing at my expense?

Although I took the brunt of the tirade, it was Universal and The Chairman who had to pick up the bill. He was given no choice but to acquiesce. *TV Guide* ripped the offending page with the listing, and Universal paid for the East Coast reprint.

Ol' Ordinary Bob blamed me for the fuck up and made sure I knew it. His low opinion of me was validated by The Chairman's blame game.

From then on, Ol' Bob had nothing good to say about me. That's the skinny anyway on the Hollywood grapevine. Ovitz knew damn well who was really to blame, but not wanting to take the heat himself, he allowed the Chairman to paint the target on my back.

I sat next to Sidney Pollack at a dinner a few months later, and I mentioned that Ol' Bob apparently hated my guts. Sidney smiled and seemed rather amused.

"Congratulations," he said as he began laughing. "If Hollywood is a war zone, then don't you think this is kinda like being awarded the Purple Heart?"

Chapter Twelve

CRY FREEDOM

The 1987 Universal release of Cry Freedom fell into the imperious category of "an important film." Translated into Hollywood-speak this often meant a socially-significant, politically-correct box office bomb.

Cry Feedom was directed by Sir Richard Attenbourough, who won two Academy Awards for the movie *Gandhi*. *Gandhi* was a brilliant biographical film based on the life of Mahatma Gandhi, leader of the nonviolent resistance against British colonial rule. Knighted by Her Majesty in 1976, for outstanding achievement in the arts, Sir Dickie as we called him, was diminutive in stature but possessed enormous presence and charm. He was an accomplished actor in his own right having starred in such major motion pictures as *The Sand Pebbles* with Steve McQueen and *Doctor Dolittle* with Rex Harrison.

Cry Freedom was set in the 1970's South African apartheid era and told the true story of the activist Steven Biko. He was arrested and subsequently beaten to death by the local police after speaking at an apartheid rally. Biko was masterfully portrayed by a young Denzel Washington. Biko's white liberal friend, journalist Donald Woods, played by actor Kevin Kline, was appalled by his friend's tragic death and sought to expose the government's involvement.

The character of Steven Biko is killed off in the first half hour of the picture. The next two hours are spent unraveling Donald Wood's travails. The re-enactment of the infamous Soweto uprising was cinematically riveting. But although intellectually interesting, most of the film is not satisfying on a visceral level. Viewing this picture I found myself wishing that Sir Dickie had made a film more about Steven Biko's extraordinary life than Wood's plight following his death. Without Denzel's presence on screen, the film lost oomph!

Columbia Pictures was the studio that released *Gandhi*. My new boss, Ed Roginski, had been second in command for Columbia's marketing division when the film broke box office records. He, along with his former staff, had formed a very tight and trusting bond with Sir Dickie. Sue, the Vice President of East Coast Publicity for Universal, was a member of this inner circle, and a breathtakingly beautiful, middle-aged woman. Sue was considered a player by industry insiders, and most importantly, by our Chairman.

Cry Freedom was the first really important film I was responsible for marketing. Sir Richard flew into L.A. for the first screening of the picture for Universal executives. I was delighted to meet Dickie, as he directed me to call him, and to spend time with such an accomplished director. The screening was followed by a luncheon to discuss potential marketing opportunities. I was anxious to hear everyone's initial thoughts about the direction we were to take with the campaign.

Unfortunately, that didn't happen.

The Chairman requested my New York counterpart be included in the lunch time meet and greet, but demanded that I be *excluded*.

To his credit, my new boss Ed Roginski didn't let The Chairman get away with this slight. As a result, both Sue and I were **uninvited.** The Chairman explained our absence to the Oscar-winning director in a way that left me with egg on my face. Sue was already established, so our no-show gave her the upper hand.

In effect, The Chairman was shooting a starter's pistol signaling the bitch fight to begin. If that was his intent, it worked. Sue and I found ourselves in an all out war. Fortunately for me, Sue made a fatal error right at the starting gate. She put her feelings about working with me in writing.

Sue, was in fact, Ed Roginski's dear friend. Even so, she was indiscreet and not known to keep secrets. So Ed never told her he was dying. During Ed's protracted illness, he needed a strong person in LA whom he could trust to take control when the time came. Sue was not on his short list—I was.

Gathering his strength, Ed, flew to New York to meet Sue for dinner at Elaine's, a famous hangout for entertainment and journalist types on the Upper East Side. It was not a pleasant evening for him. He later told me that when he arrived at the restaurant Sue was already on her second bottle of wine. She was busy making eye contact with a gentleman across the room. Her first words to Ed were, "There was a time when I could have any man I wanted. They would come across a crowded room to meet me, but not anymore..." She was in her cups and melancholy.

I felt sick to my stomach when Ed told me this story. I was sad for Sue, but also frightened for myself. Was I going to suffer Sue's pathetic fate? Was I doomed to be chronically single? An older woman in the world of youthful perfection, who wasn't perfect anymore? Was I going to play the lead in *Sunset Boulevard* for real someday?

Sue ultimately lost our little war. Two months after her dinner with Ed, The Chairman fired her and I took over.

Cry Freedom was a platform release. It opened initially on only twenty-seven screens in a few select cities. Platform openings are doubly expensive to achieve because, as the film widens out into more theaters and towns, it must be supported yet again by costly national print and television media buys.

Why a platform release? A platform release accomplishes two things. It's primarily done at the end of a year to qualify the film for Oscar consideration. Academy rules state a film must run for one week in one or more theaters to be considered for that year's Oscar nominations. Platforms also give an important film the chance to benefit from word of mouth and hopefully great reviews.

It was determined that *Cry Freedom* would open in limited release in New York, Washington D.C., Atlanta and Los Angeles on Friday, November 6th. Universal would hold premieres in each city the week before the opening. All four premieres would be attended by Sir Richard, Denzel Washington, Kevin Kline, Mr. & Mrs. The Chairman, and myself.

The first official world premiere in New York would lead off a week of touring and, as tradition dictates, take place at the Ziegfeld Theatre on West 54th Street. We'd then move to the Uptown Theatre in Washington to benefit the Robert F. Kennedy Center for Justice and Human Rights. Next we'd all head down to Atlanta to benefit the Martin Luther King Center, finally returning to Los Angeles on Thursday to wrap it all up.

I coordinated the logistics for each premiere personally. Joined by two of my senior staff, we flew into Atlanta to meet with the officials at the King Center. I never guessed at the time that day would be one of the most meaningful and educational of my life.

The King Center, located just up the street from Dr. King's tiny Ebenezer Baptist Church, is breathtaking in its simplicity. You enter the main building through "The Freedom Walkway." Designed in brick, it surrounds a tiered cascading reflection pool. Martin Luther King's (and now Coretta Scott King's) crypt lies atop the pool of tranquil blue. It reads...

"Free At Last, Free At Last, Thank God Almighty, I'm Free At Last."

In the main lobby, there is a tall, elevated glass case that displays Dr. King's clerical robe, wire-rimmed glasses, and the battered brief case that dropped from his hands as he died. I was never fortunate enough to see Dr. King in person. But along with many others, I always pictured him to be a big man physically as well as morally. I was surprised to learn that he was quite diminutive in stature. It was his commanding voice and presence that made him seem so much larger-than-life. In fact, if I'd been lucky enough to walk by his side, I would have towered over him.

My staff and I were escorted into the boardroom where we met for an hour with Dr. King's sister, Christine Ferris. She began the meeting saying a prayer. This get together was a polite formality. With most of the planning in place, there wasn't much business to discuss. Coretta Scott King arrived at the end of our meeting. Mrs. King was, in reality, lovely. She offered to show me the Ebenezer Church where Mother King had recently been assassinated. We walked together down the street. I asked her if Dr. King had ever been afraid.

"Oh yes," she said. "In the end he took pills to help with it. It wasn't dying he feared, Martin was worried that the movement would not sustain without him."

Of course, a key ally of Dr. King in the fight for equality and justice had always been Robert Kennedy. It seemed appropriate that we headed to Washington next to meet with his widow Ethel at their historic home in MacLean, Virginia known as Hickory Hill.

Ethel, looking healthy and tan, greeted us all wearing shorts and a T-shirt. She escorted us on a short tour. Before it was Robert's home, it belonged to President Kennedy and his wife Jacqueline. This was considered the Kennedy's Washington ancestral home and was filled with family photographs and mementos from international visits. I found myself gazing over the back lawn. Memories of another era came flooding back to me. How many times had I looked at magazine photographs of the family set against this backdrop of sloping green? I could almost see Brutus, their big, black Newfoundland lolling in the summer sun. Bobby was long gone and the young brood had grown up. Brutus was gone too. However, his shaggy "grandchildren" were still busy playing their version of touch football on the grass.

We walked out to the back patio. Ethel thought this was the best location for the small post-premiere dinner party she was to host for her friend Sir Dickie. She also wanted to handle hiring her caterer, ordering her wine of preference, and sending out the invitations.

Of course, everything was billed directly to Universal.

There was a well-known New York crisis management publicist by the name of John Scanlon. His claim to fame was that he had handled the horrendously screwed up General Westmoreland lawsuit in which the General filed a $120M libel case against the CBS Network. Scanlon represented the network.

John was friends with most of the national power pundits and leveraged those relationships, accepting deep-pocket money to put them together with clients who were willing to pay. This, of course, was under the umbrella of marketing. If you recall the more recent incident with Sarah Ferguson, you know that this sort of activity doesn't fly that well these days

Universal hired John Scanlon to host a chic dinner soirée scheduled the night before our New York Premiere. He comprised a guest list of elite trendsetters who would dine with Sir Dickie, our Chairman, and a few select Universal executives including myself. We hoped this group would start the buzz about how "important" the film *Cry Freedom* was.

Back in LA, the weekend before our marathon tour, I was doing a last-minute list check and realized I needed to run to the pet store and stock up on cat food. I was loading choice cans into my basket when a blue-haired lady came down the aisle escorted by "Precious," her apricot-colored toy poodle. Precious was wearing a jaunty sailor's hat and appeared damn unhappy about it. She began to growl at her Mama. Graarrrr!

Mama coo-coo'd, "Now that's a good Precious." Whereupon Precious jumped up and tried to bite her.

Mama, fractured to her very core by such hostility, dropped the leash and Precious made a run for it. The speedy little demon didn't get very far. The leash caught and wrapped around my leg. Her mama grabbed the rhinestone studded pink rope and pulled, causing it to tighten and cut off the circulation to my foot. I lost my balance and could either fall sideways which was certain to result in an ankle twist, or fall directly on Precious smashing her into Apricot jam. So I twisted my ankle.

I hopped home and called my nephew who lived close by. "I can't walk on my left foot," I reported. "Could you get me a cane?"

The next morning, my ankle, the size of a softball, I called my orthopedist and spent the better part of the morning in his office. My ankle was not broken, merely badly sprained. All taped up, I left his office with my cane and headed to my acupuncturist. The needles, carefully inserted, immediately put my ankle to sleep and it felt just dandy. When they were removed, I was back to square one.

So I went on tour aided by a cane and hobbling in a pair of ugly flat shoes. How spiffy!

John Scanlon and his wife, actress Julienne Marie, lived on the Upper West Side in a lovely but smallish apartment. It was a tight knit group in more ways than one. After the cocktail hour, the thirty plus guests were seated at round tables in the entrance hall for dinner. I enjoyed the flow of close conversation immensely. Three network anchormen were present: Tom Brokaw of NBC, Dan Rather of CBS, and Peter Jennings of ABC. *Sixty Minutes* correspondents, Mike Wallace and Morley Safer, were also there and Bryant Gumble represented *The Today Show*. Screenwriter William Goldman and *The New York Times* columnist Tom De Vries, were among the notable writers. *U.S. News & World Report* owner and publisher multi-millionaire Mort Zuckerman, the ex-boyfriend of Gloria Steinem, sat next to me. I suspected this was an attempt to replace that beautiful woman activist in this man's affections. It didn't work. There was absolutely no chemistry between us.

I was doing swimmingly accepting everyone's sympathy over my sprained ankle. While sharing a ride back to the hotel with Morley Safer he made a charming attempt at empathy. He went on to describe the time he fell over his dog while crossing a crowded Manhattan street and was taken to the hospital. "I assure you, it happens to the best of us Sally."

As I graciously accepted his kindness, The Chairman, also along for the ride, chimed in with, "Yeah, but she fell over someone else's dog. Is that stupid or what?"

On Tuesday night, the Ziegfeld Theater came alive. Klieg lights lit the sky. The red carpet ran the length of the sidewalk. Limos disgorged their famous passengers and photographers snapped away. The post-dinner reception was held directly across the street in the Hilton Hotel Grand Ballroom. At Sir Dickie's request, we flew in a large South African musical group to entertain after dinner. It was a major effort to obtain all the visas (at the last minute) and fly them and their gargantuan amount of luggage and equipment into New York. But they turned out to be worth it. Their performance was amazing. It culminated in the South African National Anthem, and was followed by a five-minute standing ovation.

The next evening, the Washington event went smoothly as well. Dinner ran late but the wine flowed during hors d'oeuvres and everyone seemed to admire the film. Senators Edward Kennedy and John Kerry each hosted a table at dinner. Ethel sat next to Sir Dickie and I had the good fortune to be seated next to Marian Wright Edelman, the first African-American woman to pass the bar exam in Tennessee. She was a former Robert Kennedy staff member and founder and head of The Children's Defense Fund. What an amazing conversation. What an amazing life. This woman quickly became my idol.

Dinner wasn't served until 10:30. Whatever the food would be, it could not top the wine that was served all evening. Ethel poured a Puligny Montrachet retailing at the time for $135 a bottle. A month later, when accounting received the invoices for this simple evening, we realized that Universal had stocked the wine cellar at Hickory Hill for some time to come. Universal was also required to pay the outlandishly large caterer's fee, and even for new stairway carpeting.

The final stop was in Atlanta where almost everything is located on Peachtree something: Boulevard, Street, Drive, Circle, or Lane. Universal maintained a field office in the heart of downtown, so I was semi-familiar with the locale. We often held word-of-mouth screenings at a theatre located on one of the Peachtrees, and we always invited a core list of dedicated moviegoers. Miss Ora and Miss Lenore were two of our regulars. In their nineties, these two great-grandmothers still referred to themselves as negro. Both had worshipped weekly with Dr. King. One of their favorite activities was to attend movie screenings and they were always delighted to stay afterwards for a glass of wine or two. The night of our Atlanta premiere was no exception.

These two ladies were the most kick-ass "sisters" I have ever met before or since. Ordinarily I stand for the entire reception. But my foot was aching so badly at one point, that I went over to their table and asked if I might join them. I pulled up another chair for my foot.

"Honey," Ora hooted, "you just ain't in good shape. You need get you some grape juice. Always works for me." With that they both rocked with laughter.

"What did ya do to yoursefs? I hopes you had some kinda fun!" They rocked and hooted some more. They were on a roll enjoying the fact that they were quickly becoming the center of attention.

The Chairman, intrigued by what was happening, joined the table

"Yo mister," Miss Lenore puffed. "What you do to this girl?" Everyone was laughing now.

As I, yet again, explained the whole pathetic story, the ladies succumbed to another glass or two of Cabernet. I still hurt but the two old gals were way beyond feeling any discomfort. This is when Miss Ora announced, "We need a healing here Reverend, yes we do."

Miss Lenore immediately joined in, "Yes indeed, we need a healing performed Reverend. Come over here right now."

Officially summoned, the Reverend Ralph Abernathy advanced to my side. The Reverend, a major leader in the Civil Rights Movement, had been Martin Luther King's closest associate and was with him when Martin was assassinated in Memphis, Tennessee.

Rev. Abernathy began by laying his hand on my ankle, directing me as if from his pulpit, "REPEAT MY WORDS: I will be healed oh Lord."

Oh my God, I was going to pee my panties. This was turning into an old-fashioned revival meeting.

"I will be healed oh Lord," I said hesitantly.

"LOUDER," Miss Ora railed.

"I will be healed oh Lord." I was laughing so hard at this point I could hardly breath. The Chairman dissolved into hysterics.

"I praise thee oh Lord for thy healing," the Reverend continued.

"I praise thee oh Lord for thy healing," I managed to blurt.

"Raise your voice in Hallelujah and Amen Sisters!"

"Hallelujah and praise the Lord forever. Amen, oh Lord, Amen. Rest your head easy tonight Reverend Ralph for you have done the Lord's work, and she will be healed." With that, everyone applauded and we all had another glass of wine.

Exhausted either from mortification or spiritualization, I fell into a deep, undisturbed slumber that night. The next day I awoke, hopped out of bed, and discovered my pain was gone. Completely gone!

Dr. and Mrs. King, Reverend Ralph Abernathy, and the grand old gals have all left us now. But sometimes I stop and shout, "Hallelujah and Amen" in their memory.

Then I have a glass of wine and remember: *"Free at last. Free at last. Almighty God they're free at last."*

Chapter Thirteen

THE HOLLYWOOD WIVES CLUB

*Here's an inside tip for ya! If you're a single woman
with a job in Hollywood, stay as far away from the
"Hollywood Wives Club" as possible. This is one
reality show that is just too frighteningly REAL.*

Hollywood wives don't have a clue what to do with all their time.
Married to alpha males, these beautiful women are often just window
dressing for some horny hound's life.

There are exceptions. But I'm talking about the ladies who, after
snagging Mr. Sugar Daddy, hiring the architect, selecting the interior designer, grilling the personal chef, road-testing the chauffeur, maligning the
manicurist, harassing the hairdresser, interviewing the personal shopper,
handling the household staff and nitpicking the nannies, are exhausted
from waking up each day with so much time on their hands.

After the requisite tennis, therapeutic massage, tanning bed, yoga,
meditation, and organic vegetable smoothie, the wife searches for a charity to occupy her time. Her philanthropic work will certainly help some
very worthwhile organization and, far more importantly, might garner her
some of her husband's precious attention and admiration. It's attention
from their spouse that these ladies crave most.

What this means to the workingwomen forced to interact with their
tubby-hubbies all day, is trouble with a capital T. The cold, hard fact is, as
her hubby's co-worker, you will be spending a lot more time with him than
his wife as he plays his master-of-the-universe games. If you are a single
woman as I was, watch out. Unless you are a lesbian, you represent a major
threat.

Usually the wife's first course of action is to get to know you. She
invites you to be friends. But a word of warning: Don't do it! Not over your

dead carcass sister! I know what I'm talking about, because I learned the hard way. My indoctrination came courtesy of The Chairman's wife.

The Chairman's wife began calling me to talk about "oh just this and that". These little spontaneous tête-à-têtes were disruptive but seemed innocent enough. When we all traveled together to premieres or film festivals, I was usually invited to dine with the happy couple. It didn't take me long to realize this was not just a simple courtesy. The Chairman relied on me to keep the conversation neutral and flowing comfortably while he zoned out. This might have been easier if The Missus was a sparkling conversationalist, but she was uncomfortable with small talk and socially inept. For me, it was just damn hard work chewing the fat, while my sautéed vegetables got cold.

The Mrs. Chairman dressed only in black or black and red. Upon greeting someone, she made a big deal out of refusing the traditional kiss-kiss because of the possibility of catching "that something," all the while boasting of her keen support of the AIDS Project Los Angeles. She made everyone uncomfortable by insisting she struggle to carry her own luggage, even onto *private* planes. This wasn't paying homage to the Jimmy Carter school of thought. She was worried someone might try to touch something of hers, and she was touch-a-phobic.

I learned through the grapevine that her first husband had killed himself. My "snarky tooth" tempts me to say that I understand completely why he'd do such a thing. My decent human side realizes that he must have had serious issues to leave behind a young wife and baby daughter. I'm sure it took some courage for this widow to move forward and marry The Chairman. Together they had two children of their own.

The Chairman was rarely home. None of us were home much really. If we were, we were on the phone. We all worked 24/7. The Mrs. Chairman felt neglected. As I was the one who worked most consistently and closely with her husband, she began to carp to me. One morning, she called me at the office to relay her previous night's conversation with her spouse who arrived home late.

"I'm pregnant," she announced as he came in the door.

"Oh, come on. Stop playing around," he snapped.

"Maybe I wouldn't be playing around if you played with me anymore," she began to cry.

Oh my God, how embarrassing. I couldn't believe she was telling me this. It's hard to render me completely speechless but I certainly was. I mumbled something about "oh you are just so funny," feigned an important call waiting, and hung up.

Two weeks later out of the blue, she messengered a gift box to me. It arrived while I was conducting a departmental staff meeting in my office. Believing it to be a simple gift, I opened it in front of the twenty or so staffers packed in the room. I had no idea what the thing I lifted from the box was until I held it up. Someone clarified, "It's a life-size, anatomically correct, male blowup doll."

I was stunned. Where the hell was I, a sleazy bachelorette party? How inappropriate could this woman get? No one in the room laughed, not even a snicker. Without a word, I opened my office door, dumped the package on my secretary's desk, and asked him please to "get rid of this in the garage dumpster, right now." I had never been so disgusted.

But this was minor compared to what came next.

A month or so later, Universal held a premiere party for Spike Lee's film, *Mo Better Blues,* starring Denzel Washington, at a small contemporary restaurant in Tribeca on the Lower East Side of NYC. It was a hot, jungle fever kind-of-night in Manhattan—humid and close. Large iced-drinks full of hooch flowed liberally and several flowed right into The Mrs. Chairman.

Swaying over to me, without warning, she plopped down at my table in the chair reserved for Denzel. I was enthusiastically engaged in a conversation about Spike's innovative work with a Universal Pictures co-executive, an editor of *Premiere* magazine and a feature writer for *People.* Interrupting our conversational roll, the Mrs. began to talk about the friendship she had developed with her eldest daughter. They were, in her slurred words "bessst friendss." Her daughter had begun to date, so mom had asked her how the sex was. When The Chairman got wind of this mother-daughter conversation, he'd apparently "hit the roof." He sternly reminded his wife that she was the mother, not a teenage friend, of their daughter, and to start acting like it.

"He'ss wrong issn't he?" she asked all of us looking blankly around the table with glazed eyes. "I mean, if she's having sshex she needs to tell me or sshe might end up having to have an abortion—like I d-did."

Okay. This was my cue to put an end to this. Sans one word exchanged between us, my associate and I escorted Mrs. Chairman to the awaiting limo, climbed in beside her, and rode with her all the way uptown. We practically had to carry her to the room. The only thing we didn't do was put her in bed and tuck her in. I don't usually provide turn-down service and a breath mint.

Later in the summer, one of the minions in my promotion department asked to speak with me. A pretty blonde girl (I deliberately call her a girl) was quickly earning herself a reputation for being trouble. She was very perky with an upturned nose and sassy figure, so usually got her way when playing her little girlish tricks.

My policy was that any staffer who asked to speak with me was always welcome, so in Miss Minion came. She had been involved with a local family charity for two years serving on their planning committee. She wanted me to know about a fundraising luncheon to honor three fathers of the year. The committee would select the honorees. My guess was anyone with enough industry clout, even Dr. Jekyll or Mr. Hyde for that matter, would be considered. Miss Minion wanted my permission to ask The Chairman to be one of the proud dads so honored.

My answer was a swift and emphatic "No." I explained that as a policy we never became involved with any sort of personal request extended to any of our executives. NEVER! In the rare case The Chairman asked us to handle a personal event for him—only then would we become involved.

Believe me. I could not have been more clear. She, on the other hand, could not have been more devious. She came back in to my office two days later.

"Oh, Sally, I just happened to run into The Chairman at lunch and, well, the father of the year thingie just popped out of me. Guess what? He said yes."

I should have fired her for insubordination. I didn't. Big BIG mistake. I called The Chairman instead.

"Are you out of your cotton pickin' mind?" I began. "You don't want to get involved in a charade like this. I have no idea how reputable this charity is. We have no idea who the other fathers will be. Hell, they could pick John Gotti for all you know!"

I was trying to be logical.

"I want to do it for my wife. She'll love it and right now I need her to love something. It will be good for her."

This was rife with disaster.

I checked out the charity. It was a legitimate little civic organization. Their board finally locked in three recipients of their coveted prize. Honorees were: singer Wayne Newton, sports agent legend "show me the money" Leigh Steinberg, and our own dear Chairman.

Miss Minion explained that all each honoree had to do was put together a short montage video of the kids bonding with dad and show up with the family for the lunch. Period.

"Okay" I warned her. "You alone, up close and personal, handle this with Mrs. Chairman and get it done correctly. I want daily reports on your progress. "Do you u-n-d-e-r-s-t-a-n-d this time?"

"Oh yes ma'am," she said convincingly.

Not surprisingly, there wasn't any home footage of the Chairman playing with the kids. It didn't exist. So Mrs. Chairman decided to bring all three kids to the studio, hire a video crew, and have them make a nice speech about their father to the camera. This sounded workable to me.

The entire entourage arrived and decided to use my office as their green room. There they lounged all afternoon watching TV and eating M&Ms, making it impossible for me to do my work. The Mrs. had written a script for each child to read while wearing Groucho Marx moustache glasses. The big joke was that the missus thought The Chairman looked a bit like Groucho. Personally, I thought he resembled Einstein more than cute ol' Groucho.

The kids were impatient, camera shy, embarrassed, and displayed no talent. The scripts tried way too hard to be clever, sassy, and snide rather than sincere about dear old dad. The glasses were an awkward prop, and each kid's segment ran about three minutes. This was going to be just awful. Mrs. Chairman, however, seemed quite happy with the footage of her three beasts. She even sent me five bags of M&Ms the next day with a note thanking me for my time. Fortunately, they weren't wrapped in another gift box.

If only the story ended here, but of course it doesn't.

Unbeknownst to me, Miss Minion conferred in private with Mrs. Chairman, and they agreed to let the video crew make tiny edits to the footage as long as the missus would have final approval of the edited piece before the luncheon.

Tiny changes morphed into major cuts. Nine minutes was cut down to three. Why so drastic? Because Miss Minion had gleaned at the eleventh hour that each video was only to be three minutes in length maximum.

Did she tell me this? No.

Did she inform Mrs. Chairman of the necessary drastic changes? No.

Did she even show the final edit to her? HELL FUCKING NO!

The morning of the lunch I checked with Miss Minion to make sure she had gone over the program with The Chairman, that he was comfortable with everything, and that he was one hundred percent prepared. She affirmed he was completely up to date and ready to go. She also confirmed that a limo would pick up the Mrs. and kids. She explained The Chairman had opted to drive himself and wanted me to ride in the suicide seat.

This was one time I should have been smart enough not to wear my seatbelt.

Universal Pictures had purchased four very expensive tables filled to capacity with industry guests. Miss Minion accounted for each body and where they were to sit. She carefully provided me with a copy of her seating chart, so that I could make the rounds at each table and greet everyone.

The Chairman and I arrived late and wandered through the hotel lobby intending to meet up with Mrs. Chairman and the kiddies. We found her throwing her usual hissy fit. The charity provided corsages for all the wives, but the Mrs. did not care to wear "one of those tacky things." Saved from most of this drama by our tardiness, The Chairman was snatched away and escorted to his place of honor on the dais. Out of four possible tables, I was unfortunately seated with the family. I wanted to connect with Miss Minion, but she was nowhere to be seen. I soon realized she was AWOL. The long anticipated awards ceremony began, and it was too late to track her down.

First up was Leigh Steinberg. This hard-nosed sports agent was adorable on the home video playing football with his kids. While accepting his award, he made heartfelt spontaneous remarks about the joys of fatherhood.

Wayne Newton, hair dyed coal black and slicked back with carburetor grease was typical Mr. Vegas. He showed photos of his little princess horseback riding on their ranch. Naturally, he ended his remarks with a warm rendition of *Danke Schoen* and a touring schedule of his upcoming appearances.

Then it was The Chairman's turn. The butchered video rolled and from frame one made no sense whatsoever. The kids had been inter-cut into a complete shambles and what in heaven's name was this Groucho thing? No one even smiled. If smoke could actually come out of someone's ears, then Mrs. Chairman would have looked like a forest fire. To add insult to fatal injury, The Chairman had nothing scripted to say about his kids or fatherhood. Believe me, he is not an extemporaneous speaker by nature. He fumbled so badly, I couldn't bear to watch the painful scene.

Lunch over, our four tables snuck away as the Mrs. turned to me and said, "I don't like surprises" with much the same tone as, "it isn't nice to fool mother nature!" She then stormed out without a word to anyone, three cowering kids in tow.

I was curbside when The Chairman's car pulled forward. This time I consciously decided to buckle myself in and tighten the strap. Hang on, honey, we were in for a bumpy ride. Boy, oh boy, did he let me have it with both barrels blazing. No joke. He ripped me a new one.

"This was for her. She was supposed to be happy. She isn't happy, so I'm not happy."

"Neither am I," I began quietly. "But at the risk of losing my life, may I remind you, I begged you not to do this. I fucking begged you. If you don't listen to me then you are partly to blame for what happens. I'm damn tired of being put in the middle." (I thought about adding, "The middle of you and your wife's problems" but didn't.)

"Fire that little bitch," he said.

"I have no problem doing that," I assured him. "But let's be clear it's not because she's the only one to blame here. I will fire her for insubordination." I was losing it. I could hear the shrill tone in my voice but I couldn't shut up, "I instructed her NOT to ask you to participate in this. She went ahead and did it anyway. Then I begged you NOT to get into this. You did anyway. Now look at the result: A young mother (Ms. Minion was a single mom) loses her job and you blame me. Your wife mercifully won't speak to me again, and in your mind everything is solved. Well, just for the record, it isn't."

True to my word, Miss Minion was out. The Mrs. felt humiliated and held me responsible, despising me from that day forward. She wasted huge amounts of her time and energy doing so.

There is no doubt in my mind that our "Lady Macbeth" was the deep throat responsible for some particularly vicious rumors circulated about me. Including the absurd notion that I was having an affair with her husband. The Chairman himself told me about that one. He informed me that an acquaintance of his told him about the rumor, to which he replied, "I should be so lucky."

I told him that I would just have laughed it off.

"Bitch," he said.

To this day I hate the sight of M&Ms.

Chapter Fourteen

BORN ON THE FOURTH OF JULY

I read the book Born on the Fourth of July several times. In the book,
Ron Kovic described his war experiences in a way that inspired pathos.
The film, directed by Oliver Stone, inspired raw anger. Born on the
Fourth of July would be a tough picture to market.

I met Tom Cruise when we both attended the initial full-cut screening of *Born On The Fourth of July* (BOFJ) directed by Oliver Stone. Sorry
to say, I wasn't blown away by his star appeal. He's one of many in Hollywood who photograph far better than they look in person. At the time, he
was still married to his first wife, actress Mimi Rogers, who tagged along
for the evening. They lacked that positive vibe you would expect from a
young couple. By the end of that year, they split, and in April the following
year Nicole Kidman entered the picture.

BOFJ is the autobiographical story of Ron Kovic, a patriotic, small-
town kid played by Tom Cruise. Ron was taught to believe that fighting for
his country was his duty. So following graduation from high school, Ron
immediately joined the U.S. Marine Corps. He served two tours of duty in
Vietnam. His last tour ended when he was critically wounded in battle. His
injuries left him permanently wheelchair-bound. Returning home with a
Bronze Star for Valor and a Purple Heart, the boy confronts a changing
and hostile world.

The film script is an adaptation of Kovic's best-selling autobiography of the same name. Kovic penned the screenplay with Oliver. Oliver
was very close to the subject matter, being a disillusioned veteran of war
himself. He enlisted in the Army, fought with the 25th Infantry Division,
and then moved on to the First Cavalry Division. He was also awarded the
Bronze Star and the Purple Heart.

BOFJ was the second in Oliver's trilogy of films about the Vietnam era. The series began with *Platoon* and eventually ended with *Heaven & Earth.* Many critics later praised BOFJ as the most ambitious and best non-documentary film ever made about the Vietnam experience.

Personally, I found this picture almost unbearable to watch. I grew up in the eclectic, free-spirited 60's of Berkeley, California. Along with legions of my generation, I actively protested the war. I once stood outside the Century Plaza Hotel in Los Angeles shouting "Hell no! We won't go!" at the Presidential caravan carrying Richard Nixon to a Republican fundraising dinner. I was a Eugene McCarthy volunteer in Chicago for the 1968 Democratic Convention. I watched many of my friends go out to protest the war, only to come back with their heads smashed and bloodied by police batons.

Oliver knew about my background. I watched the initial screening of BOFJ with him. When the theatre lights came up, he walked directly over to me.

"So, did I get it right?" he queried.

"Yes," was my immediate answer.

He got *it* very right. And because he did, *it* was a painful and grueling experience to sit through. It seemed like Oliver had directed this film to punish rather than embrace the viewer.

Oliver Stone and Tom Cruise had a mutual press agent, one tough lady by the name of Andrea Jaffe. Industry outsiders don't realize that mega stars rarely pay for anything—even their own publicists. Motion picture studios typically pay for a big star's publicist. Ironically, the publicists' primary job is to protect their client from the studio executive "suits" as they are also known.

It was six months before the opening of BOFJ, and I had yet to meet Andrea face-to-face. So I set up a meet and greet lunch. I hoped we would work together to implement a comprehensive, coordinated campaign to motivate the widest possible audience to see the film. A friendly lunch seemed a good place to start.

My guileless goal was stymied dramatically when my boss, The Chairman, called me early the day of my scheduled lunch with Andrea demanding that I, "Fire Andrea Jaffe immediately!"

He was livid because she "allowed" *The LA Times* to run a "Sunday Magazine" cover story on the filming of BOFJ. Although a cover story is usually considered a coup, The Chairman considered this article written entirely from the wrong point of view. He felt it should have been held until he personally gave her the green light to publish.

First off, let's be clear. One does not *allow* a major newspaper to do anything. One negotiates for placement and more often than not you get screwed. If the editors want to move a story up, then they move it up. Secondly, any first-year PR101 student knows you can't fire Tom Cruise and Oliver Stone's personal publicist and get away with it—not for any reason —especially not for doing her job.

The Chairman was painfully aware that this film might be a tough market. It wasn't like Oliver's previous venture, *Platoon,* which had legs of its own. I read this latest directive as a way for him to pick-a-fight so he could throw his studio weight around, hoping to take control over the marketing. This tactic may have worked on a group of public relations and marketing newbies, but not with these honchos.

"Oliver was the one who gave his personal green light to the *Times* story before he turned the film over to us," I explained to The Chairman. "You want me to fire him, too?"

"No, I want you to fire her," he yelled, "or fire yourself."

Tempting!

Andrea was already seated at a booth in the Universal Commissary when I arrived. "Hi, I'm Sally," I said cheerfully.

"Andrea," she said as we shook hands.

"So Andrea," I said jovially, "you're fired. The Chairman is very mad at you for the story yesterday which, by the way, was fabulous."

"Oh," she replied buttering her roll. "So now what are we going to talk about?"

"What's the latest gossip?" was the only thing I could think of except talk about the weather, which I always find so boring. It was LA after all.

Just then The Chairman entered the room and tried to sneak past our table unnoticed. No way, Jose'! I stood up and waved him over, making large gestures with my arms. No one in the room could miss my summons, and he had no choice but to come over. I figured he would join us and waste some of his own damn time, too. Andrea was ignoring me as I attempted to facilitate a polite introduction.

"I guess after lunch I'm going to have to call Tom and Oliver," said Andrea to no one in particular.

The Chairman, imitating a complete putz—oh I forgot, he was a complete putz—tossed a few weak verbal punches in Andrea's direction, but she just smiled pleasantly. This threw The Chairman completely off his game of intimidation, so he spun on his heels and left.

"Waiter, can I have the reality check please?"

I have no doubt phone calls were exchanged that afternoon. The results came as expected. Andrea not only remained on the job, but received a raise as an enticement to stay.

This unusual beginning served to bond a friendship between Andrea and me. It turned out we worked fairly well together, too. This was a surprise to almost everyone, because we are both such direct, outspoken women. Normally, two strong personalities in Hollywood never mix. Early in the process we decided that I'd basically handle Oliver and she'd handle Tom. This worked out great! I had grown fond of Oliver in spite of his often morose attitude and tendency to fly off the handle at any given moment.

Such a moment arrived a few weeks later during a morning phone call.

"You have personally fucked my film," he spewed his accusation in my direction, "by allowing that bitch Pauline Kael into last night's New York press screening."

I *personally* did no such thing. His early morning call reached me in LA, and that's exactly where I was the previous night. My location, of course, made it impossible for me to be culpable. But that didn't stop Oliver from screaming that I had "ruined his picture" and that I was "obviously working for Pravda."

"Now that annoys me Oliver," I defended myself, "because I am certainly not working for the official newspaper of the Russian Communist

Party (Pravda). I work for Universal."

Mad as he was, he did manage to laugh. "Same difference," he said.

I promised I would get hold of my New York office immediately and suss out the facts. The truth was that Kael, the preeminent movie critic for the *New Yorker* magazine and author of several critically acclaimed books about film, had simply shown up, unannounced, to our invitation only screening. My staff had determined that, in light of her status, politically they had to let her in. Kael was a pro. She knew why she hadn't been invited to the screening and she knew no one would have the balls to block her way in when she showed up.

Kael was not on our screening list because she consistently irritated Oliver. She'd never been complimentary about his work. In fact, she had a nasty habit of hating his movies and BOFJ was no exception. She dismissed this picture in her *New Yorker* review by stating "Oliver Stone's movie yells at you for two hours and twenty-five minutes."

She wasn't the only critic, professional or not, to feel this way. An enraged acquaintance of my mother's actually wrote to me directly at the studio, "You ought to be ashamed to have anything to do with a movie that rants and shows those horrible things." Interestingly, it wasn't the soldiers' deaths that bothered her. She was mainly referring to the graphic hospital colostomy scenes and the Mexican brothels.

"Real life is tough," I wrote back. "This is what war does to people."

However, her note did remind me of a great line from the popular comedy *Butterflies Are Free,* which was first a Broadway play and then a movie starring Goldie Hawn. The mother and daughter are having a disagreement about a play they had recently seen.

"But motherrr," the daughter whines, "it's part of life."

"So is diarrhea, but I wouldn't classify it as entertainment," the mother replies.

In much the same way, it was also difficult to classify BOFJ as entertainment. It was a profoundly leveling and disturbing experience. Yet most who saw it recognized that, although cruelly raw, Oliver's direction was a brilliant incursion into unchartered cinematic waters. And Cruise's performance as the disillusioned boy forced to become a martyr to his own country was exemplary.

The film opened in limited theaters on December 20, 1989. The revenues were dismal. We immediately began an aggressive and very costly *Academy Award* nomination campaign. Academy voters, at this time, were still required to view the films in a legitimate theater before voting. These days, many just watch advance screening DVDs in the comfort of their easy chairs at home. I feel this dilutes the movie experience altogether.

Beginning in January of 1990, Universal held screenings every night at our three-hundred-seat onsite Alfred Hitchcock theater. A pre-screening buffet dinner was served in our commissary as a convenience and incentive to attend the film. We ran daily full-page industry trade publication ads in *Variety* and *The Hollywood Reporter,* a vanity expense in the high six-figures.

The *Golden Globes* had become in recent years a huge indicator of which films and actors would earn the Oscar nod six weeks later. So our foreign publicity office wined and dined the International press based in Los Angeles who had voting privileges on *Golden Globe* nominations.

The *Globes* greatly encouraged us that year. Tom Cruise was nominated for Best Actor and won. Oliver was awarded Best Director and BOFJ was named Best Picture of the Year. We felt we were on our way to Oscar victory. Even so, we were still taking a beating at the box office. The weekly reports were dismal.

Instead of flocking to see BOFJ, audiences across the country headed in droves to see a feel good charmer called *Driving Miss Daisy* starring the beguiling Jessica Tandy and an equally compelling Morgan Freeman. *Daisy's* box office take was huge and money talks BIG TIME in Hollywood, especially to the keepers of Oscar gold.

Popping up to the forefront in the Best Actor's category was the lovely English-Irish actor, Daniel Day-Lewis, who turned in a mesmerizing performance as a handicapped man in a little film entitled, *My Left Foot.* He was the critic's choice in this category. Truth be told, he was my odds-on favorite, too.

The Academy announced the nominations at five in the morning Pacific Standard Time. It was scheduled at this hellish hour so the announcement could be covered live on the East Coast by network morning news programs. Publicists, studio reps, and agents flocked to the site where, two minutes before the camera lights turned from red to green, Academy personnel handed out the printed, multi-page list of nominations. This amounted to a feeding frenzy terrifying to watch. Then, in a mad rush to the pay phones (cell phones were uncommon in 1990), people fought to break the news to their clients before anyone else. Good news is always great. But if the news was bad, they would need to spin it in such a way so as to keep their jobs.

Phones rang all over the world that morning. Champagne corks popped. Even at that early hour, Universal Studios consumed a great deal of Cristal.

I received a call from my onsite vice president of publicity. *Born on the Fourth of July* had received eight Academy nominations including Best Picture, Best Director, Best Actor, and Best Film editing!

Immediately I placed my call to The Chairman. He was generally grumpy in the morning, but given the amazing news, he couldn't think of anything snarky to say. He managed to croak out, "Well done."

I didn't call Oliver because Andrea was his publicist. It was appropriate that she be the first to tell him. Still, I was touched when he called me later. He was very generous in his praise and said that from now on he would fondly refer to me as Pravda. He hoped I intended to wear red to the Oscars.

I had my fingers crossed Oscar night. Billy Crystal was again the host for the evening. His opening monologue was always the best part of the endless hours we had to spend in a freezing theater awaiting our fate. I arrived early to be on hand to help Oliver and Tom navigate dozens of interviewers lining the red carpet. This is when the requisite hugs and kisses and good lucks go on between nominees while press agents jockey for camera time. Finally everyone takes their seats.

I had to visit the ladies room during one of the commercial breaks. At the Oscars, while you're out of your seat, they place what is known as a filler (a live body) in it so the theater always looks full. Truthfully, while all the techie awards were handed out most of the non-celebrities—those not camera worthy—usually hung out in the lobby where it's much warmer.

I was late returning from the ladies room and found myself locked out of the theater until the next break. The ceremony had finally reached the big awards so the lobby was empty now except for one tall, thin, dark-haired lurch of a guy wearing what appeared to be a morning coat and a ribbon tie. As he nervously lit his fourth cigarette in three minutes, I decided to go over and see if I could talk to him and perhaps calm him down.

"Hey," I began, "I'm Sally from Universal and I just want you to know that if there is a God in Hollywood, you would win tonight. But, let's face it, there isn't, so don't sweat it."

He laughed, the doors opened and we went in to sit down. That tall, thin fellow was Daniel Day-Lewis and minutes later he did in fact win the Oscar for Best Actor. I was thrilled for him. His performance in *My Left Foot* was flawless, and he deserved the Academy Award.

As I suspected, *Driving Miss Daisy* won for Best Picture. Even though BOFJ did not win a sweep of the Oscars, Oliver was awarded Best Director. Film critic Roger Ebert wrote the next day that, "Oliver Stone directed a picture that speaks to the philosophical core of war. It is not a movie about battle but about an America that changed its mind about the war."

During the Christmas of 1989, I spotted a small bronze sculpture of an antelope in a shop window. She was a serene delicate creature with one leg stretched out in front and one tucked under her. She was peacefully resting. For some unfathomable reason she made me think of Oliver. On a whim, I had it wrapped and sent to him.

In return, I received a "rare for me" handwritten note from Oliver Stone thanking me for the, "wounded antelope sculpture which now sits on my piano."

Oliver saw a figure as wounded. I saw her as serene. With that brief note, which I will always keep, I discovered an insight into the mystery of an Oliver Stone few others are allowed to see. I found Oliver to be brilliant, difficult, stubborn, rash, arrogant, dark, moral, caring, sweet, and completely compelling. A conflicted wounded old soul himself, I

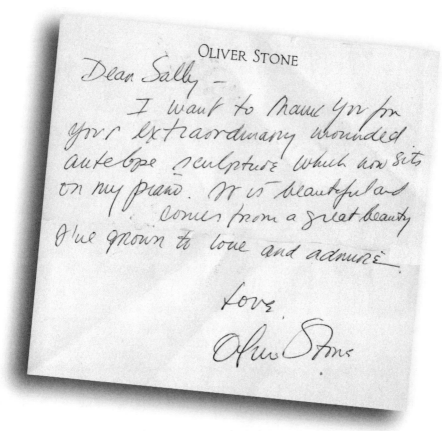

OLIVER STONE

Dear Sally –

I want to thank you for your extraordinary wounded antelope sculpture which now sits on my piano. It is beautiful and comes from a great beauty I've grown to love and admire.

Love,

Oliver Stone

Thank you note from Oliver Stone.

believe Oliver Stone will always be a passenger on his own private *Midnight Express.*

If you have never seen the film *Midnight Express* you should. Oliver Stone wrote the script. It is brilliant.

Regrettably, I never had the opportunity to work with him again.

Chapter Fifteen

THE MOBSTERS

Bugsy Siegel once said, "Class, that's the only thing that counts in life. Class. Without class and style, a man's a bum. He might as well be dead."

Paramount Pictures brought you *The Untouchables* starring Kevin Costner, Sean Connery and Robert De Niro. Warner Brothers, in association with Martin Scorsese, brought you *Goodfellas* starring Robert De Niro, Joe Pesci and Ray Liotta. Tri-Star released *Bugsy* with Warren Beatty and Annette Bening. Not to be outdone, our consigliere bootlegged *The Mobsters.* You remember this one don't you? You don't? Must be because the critics put their own contract out on the movie and its stars Christian Slater, Costas Mandylor, and Dr. McDreamy himself—Patrick Dempsey.

The Mobsters was short on style and without any class whatsoever. It went straight to video or should I say *The Mobsters* was put on ice. Mowed down in cold blood. Deep-sixed with cement shoes. Or as Mickey Blue would say, "Forget about it. "

I first met our less than stellar cast at a dinner in New York at Cipriani's, located in the Pierre Hotel. This venue is a knock-off of the famous Harry's Bar in Venice, Italy and is owned and managed by the same Italian family. Patrick Dempsey, now the beloved sex symbol of *Grey's Anatomy,* was still a young actor at the time, only a kid really. He was married to his manager, a hardened, middle-aged, trigger lady, appropriately named Rocky, who didn't look like she'd be anyone's moll. Meeting this version of Patrick made it damn near impossible to imagine him cultivating the "most sexy man ever image" he has today. Back then, he was a nice-looking shadow for his momma mia running the show.

Like any Guido could tell ya, this was not the most stimulating group of actors with whom to dine, much less make a movie with. I was glad old Rocky tagged along, because at least she kept the conversation flowing. Like, you know, pass the cannolies and stuff. Rocky took care of her own, so Patrick never had to ask for anything. I remember thinking Patrick must be running some kind of a racket on the side, cuz this sure was an odd pair. Thank God, Cipriani's makes a hell of a Bellini (a mix of Peach Nectar and the Italian sparkling wine Prosecco), so at least I managed to stay hydrated throughout this family meal.

Christian Slater brought his overbearing publicist whose name I can't recall. The memory lapse is intentional on my part, because she was a complete and utter bitch. Throughout the marketing process for this film, which had severe limitations, she made a complete fool of herself. One of her more transparent demands was that I book her and Christian adjoining suites, because, she confided, "Christian suffered dreadfully from nightmares and needs me close by for support and comfort."

Oh whatever, doll. Just be sure to slam the door shut.

Costas Mandylor was the nicest of the three actors. But who'd ever heard of the guy before or, for that matter, since?

After dinner, we headed home to decide what thrust our publicity campaign would take. We had to decide on a direction even before seeing the film. This was not unusual, for we often relied on notes, trailers and scripts when still in production. The question was, "What can we do that will garner attention for what we hope will be an epic gangland drama?"

A quick polling of the press revealed a palatable *lack* of interest in our stars and almost none in the movie. It wasn't personal, just business. So we decided it might increase the public's appetite if we hosted a premiere for the film at the New York Supper Club on West 47th and Broadway, the closest venue to real Mafia turf we could secure. To entice others to the gathering, I invited some notable associates. In this mix were Bob Guccione, founder of *Penthouse Magazine* and John Gotti, head of the Gambino crime family, who had just been indicted on racketeering charges and five counts of murder. This was to be a select group. We threw in Donald Trump for good measure, too.

The invitations needed to be an offer they couldn't refuse, so my staff and I brainstormed and came up with the perfect "summons." It was a dead fish wrapped in newspapers—a bit odorous but uniquely memorable. We hired out-of-work actors to dress up as old-world gangsters to do our legwork. They rang doorbells all over town and, as our unsuspecting invitee opened the front door, a "package" was thrust into their hands. In a menacing voice they announced, "Big Willie says to be there." Doormen were an obstacle. But when they heard, "Your old friend Mickey sent us," and we greased their palms with some scratch, most of these guardian angels helped us locate the targeted apartments.

Of course, some doors were slammed in our face. For instance, we tried to deliver an invitation to anchorman Forrest Sawyer at ABC. But he refused to accept it, saying he was currently busy working on an exposé of Scientology. Besides, he thought our invitation smelled fishy. I heard, however, that Donald Trump got a real bang out of it. Our actor tracked him down in the Plaza Hotel's famous Oak Room seated with girlfriend Marla Maples. Good thing The Donald owned the joint or some poor actor might have gotten himself clipped.

My staff and I were having fun with our little publicity stunt up until we screened the picture. That's when we decided to hire a hit man to shoot us all. This flick was a flop. It was not even funny awful, just plain awful. Patrick Dempsey played the mob's Jewish accountant Meyer Lansky with all the appeal of a dead rat. Christian Slater was Lucky Luciano with a high falsetto voice. The script was convoluted and confusing. Who was Costas Mandylor supposed to be? Had anyone in the production department actually read this drivel?

The Chairman was so beside himself after the initial screening, he was rendered speechless. Bright and early the next morning, I was summoned to his office. Even though the New York premiere was only one week away, he wanted it cancelled. We were already booked and locked with invitations out. His request was understandable, but I felt it imperative to point out that such an abrupt cancellation would signal to the press that we had a bomb on our hands. The question was which alternative was worse: call off the premiere and let them print that they suspected a bomb, or go forward and hope there was one critic who might say something positive?

Who was the boss who said "Better that your enemies overestimate your stupidity than your shrewdness?"

When all else fails, I always say go for the completely implausible.

I surmised if we showed the film, it would certainly ruin the very creative evening we had planned. So yes, my friends, we proceeded to hold a wonderful premiere for *The Mobsters* without actually screening the movie.

How's that for brass with a brand new spin? This movie is so special, we aren't even going to show it to you!

Stagers dressed the Supper Club in what I can only describe as early Art Deco style meets Little Italy. The band played famous songs of the 40's, *Sentimental Journey, Stormy Weather...Paper Doll.* Bob Guccione showed up and held court with a table full of Penthouse playmates. Gotti begged off, citing a previous engagement at Riker's Island. Trump arrived with soon-to-be second wife Marla Maples with her mother and sister in tow. This foursome was well guarded by two seriously huge goons who I think must once have been part of *the family.*

The celebrated *Detroit Free Press* entertainment columnist, Shirley Eder, decided to fly up for the family gig. Shirley's real-life husband owned a meat packing company (Hormel sounds familiar). This little known fact highly amused her because she thought it made him sound like a heavy who probably had his nose broken more than once. She referred to him as, "My husband the meat packer."

When Donald Trump arrived, Shirley instantly grabbed me by the collar and insisted I get him for her. It turned out to be a fairly simple assignment. The Donald and Marla were delighted to see Shirley because during their adulterous affair, she'd been the only "nice" columnist writing about their tryst. Their affair ended Donald's lengthy marriage to first-wife Ivana and raised more than a few eyebrows. As I escorted them over to the meat packer's wife, the palm of my hand accidentally brushed across Donald's bodyguard's jacket revealing, to my dismay, that the big fella was packing a big, big heater. Don't mess with this guy.

During their lengthy chat with Shirley, never a woman to shrink from the big boys, Donald and Marla began to figure out that they were not at a particularly A-list type of soirée. Not pleased, The Donald and Marla made a speedy getaway by ducking out the back alley door, leaving me in charge of a ditched mother and sister for the rest of the evening.

Not one of the actors in the film made an appearance at the party.

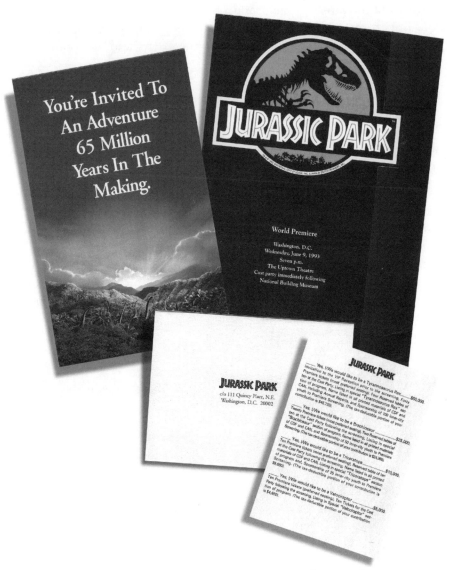

Studios spend small fortunes on promoting their movies.
Their events are often lavish to the extreme. An example of this
is the Washington, DC Presidential World Premiere
of Jurassic Park which Sally coordinated to
benefit "The Children's Defense Fund".
The movie was actually screened this evening.

Neither did the director, the producer, The Chairman, or anyone else involved with the actual making of this picture. It was just us marketing chickens and a bunch of "who knew who they were" and "who cares."

Forget about it!

You know what? The hundreds of guests who stayed did not seem to care that we never premiered the film! Later the critics followed suit and didn't bother reviewing it much either. Maybe a short, terrible mention here and there, but that was pretty much the sum total. Two thumbs down and on to the next film.

As far as I know, we are the only studio not to show the film at its premiere. We were the first and I'm pretty sure the last. Unfortunately, one must always pay the piper one way or another. For me, as a proud professional woman, the punishment for my crime of bad film association came during a lull in my evening's duties. I was approached by Bob Guccione who asked me to dance. This proved to be an all time low in my personal history of unthinkable moments. There was no way to get out of it gracefully or otherwise. So I did my version of a foxtrot with Mr. *Penthouse Magazine.*

Yuck. Gnarly!

Where the hell was Bugsy Siegal when a liberated woman needed a class act?

Chapter Sixteen

THE MUHAMMAD ALI EFFECT

In the entertainment industry the African American community
of incomparably talented men and women are beloved for
their champion spirit—they have led the way up
the mountainside....

Some of the best of the best people I have ever met belong to the African American Hollywood community. It was and is comprised of such talents as Bill Cosby, Sidney Poitier, Sammy Davis Jr., Harry Belafonte, Ozzie Davis, Barry Gordy, and Cicely Tyson. These artists forged a new path of equal opportunity for African Americans in a tough industry where the odds were stacked against them. This distinguished group would later be joined by Spike Lee, Denzel Washington, Eddie Murphy, Halle Berry, Oprah Winfrey, Whoopi Goldberg and many others. In my opinion, the most honorable member of this group is Muhammad Ali.

However, there is one member of this auspicious family who remained hidden behind the scenes until he appeared on the July 13, 1998 cover of *Sports Illustrated,* his arms draped around Muhammad Ali's shoulders. The headline read: "WHO IS THIS MAN WITH HOWARD BINGHAM? You don't know Muhammad Ali until you know his best friend."

Howard Bingham is a world-class photographer. You might remember him as a witness for the prosecution during the O.J. Simpson trial. Apparently, Howard ran into O.J. while boarding the same plane the night of the infamous murder. Since he had spoken with the defendant, he was asked to testify about that conversation.

For me, Howard would become more than just a world-class photographer. For me, he became the common thread binding all these legends together.

In 1990, Universal released a film entitled *Ghost Dad.* Directed by Sidney Poitier, the picture starred Bill Cosby who portrays just what the name implies—a ghost dad. When the audience first meets this character, he is the typical workaholic father paying no attention to his two kids. He unexpectedly dies and returns to haunt the children, this time around, paying far more attention than they need or want.

The picture was shot almost entirely on the Universal Backlot which was terrific for me. Bill Cosby had a fabulous personal chef, a small southern black woman who was a comfort food genius. Several times during production, Bill invited some of my staff and me to have lunch with him in his bungalow. The food was always wonderful. This woman made the best tamale pie I've ever eaten. As good as the food was, it was the conversation—or rather Cosby's monologues—that kept us in stitches and asking for seconds. I'm sure he was testing his material out on us, and we were more than willing to be his guinea pigs.

What you see on television is what you get with Bill Cosby. He's just fabulous. Bill was on a diet during filming, attempting to make up for the extra pounds he blissfully gained recently from enjoying great restaurants in the south of France. Bill would munch on leafy greens and riff on about one thing or another as we sat soaking it in. His hour-long break often stretched to two hours.

Sidney Poitier, on the other hand, generally worked through lunch. A serious man, he once confided to me that, "I won't do any interview that can be broken into meaningless sound bites, or one that isn't printed in the *New York Times*." In other words, Sydney did not like doing interviews. I adored him anyway. He is a lovely man with impeccable manners.

Frankly, studio expectations were never very high for this picture. It was given the green light simply because it was Poitier and Cosby. Who wouldn't want to work with this pair? Nevertheless, I was instructed to keep a tight reign on my marketing budget.

I intended to follow orders until this unit photographer (some unknown guy named Howard Bingham) was shoved down my throat by our famous duo. I didn't like that one bit. I didn't know his work, and he cost too damn much. It is difficult enough in my business to stay on budget. To redistribute monies usually means that something else suffers. It was equally difficult to say no to Sidney and Bill. No—make that impossible.

On top of having to "OK" this unforeseen expense, there was the annoying inconvenience of this Howard guy always hanging out in the publicity department located just one floor down from my office. Practically every day he'd call or stop by my secretary's desk to see if I was available to say hello. I never was, but he just wouldn't take the hint. There was no way I was making time for this guy.

Yes, I was behaving like a self-important, ego-driven studio executive jerk. In the movie business, you can contract the "jerk virus" if not careful. Fortunately for me, I would receive a quick inoculation.

One evening, my secretary had left for the day and my office door was wide open. I was on the phone at my desk when this big black-bearded man strolled in and sat down uninvited. The nerve of this idiot. I felt like yelling "get the hell out" at the top of my lungs, but he seemed very comfortable slouched in my chair and it looked like I would have to take this "unscheduled" meeting. I was on the phone a full five-minutes more before I finally hung up. It was Howard Bingham who then stood up to shake my hand. Who knew the pleasure would be all mine?

For the next two hours Howard fascinated, charmed and amazed his way into my heart where he remains tucked away to this day.

I discovered Howard was the first black photographer hired on by *Life Magazine.* One of his very first assignments was to photograph black militant Huey Newton and the newly formed Marxist group called the Black Panthers. The Panthers were headquartered in Oakland, California, literally next door to Berkeley where I grew up. I'd been exposed to many of the individual members of the Panthers and certainly knew all about their infamous leader Huey Newton.

On the numerous occasions that Newton was arrested by the Oakland police for disturbing the peace, manslaughter and murder, Howard Bingham was the only photographer allowed in the cell to photograph the prisoner. One of the photographs he took became the "official" portrait of Newton. It was a strong militant pose that captured the intensity of this self-proclaimed military leader.

I admitted to Howard that I'd always been fascinated by Newton and a little afraid of him as well. However, as a former journalist, I would have walked over hot coals for the opportunity to interview him just once before he was gunned down by a drug dealer on the streets of Oakland in

August of 1989. Even more than I wanted to meet Huey Newton, there was a non-violent Muslim leader I was desperate to someday meet.

In the late 70's, soon after I became a page at Metromedia, I was working the revival of the once popular *Steve Allen Talk Show,* answering phones and running messages back and forth. One afternoon, I went backstage to the dressing room area to locate someone, and found the guy in question talking with Allen's first guest, Muhammad Ali. Before I could react to sighting this legend, the door opened behind me and a group of young boys and girls, somewhere between the ages of seven and nine, paraded in an orderly single file into the hallway.

When the kids spotted Ali they broke rank and went wild. Not the least bit shy, they clapped and cheered at the top of their lungs while racing up to give the big man a hug. It was wonderful to see these kids express pure joy so easily. Ali hugged the kids right back. It was impossible to tell who was happier to see whom. He lifted each wiggling torso into the air. He mock punched and ducked. Every kid followed his lead. They had Ali's full attention, and he had theirs. It was a moment I will never forget. Pure magic.

I can't remember what sparked this memory while talking with Howard, but I found myself telling him this story and asking if by chance he happened to see Ali's late night appearance on the *Arsenio Hall Show* earlier in the week? Without waiting for a reply, I explained how I was touched when the champ volunteered his recipe for life: "You take a cup of love, a tablespoon of patience and a teaspoon of tolerance—mix it all up and spread it liberally around the world."

When I finally finished, Howard looked at me strangely. To cover my discomfort, I asked him, "Do you understand what I mean?"

"Yes, I do," he said. "I was with Ali at Arsenio's. I guess nobody told you, he's my best friend."

Nobody had. Somebody on my staff must have told somebody, but no one had told me. I hate being the last one to know, especially something that, as part of the movie-suit mafia, I really needed to know. Turns out, Bill Cosby was Howard's other best friend! I hadn't known that either.

"Well," Howard explained. "The truth is I have always been secretly in love with Bill's wife Camille; I just put up with him to be with her."

In fact, a few years later Cosby asked Howard to accompany their son Ennis's body home to New York after he was brutally murdered on Mulholland Drive in Los Angeles. I'd call that a best friend.

At this point in our conversation it was getting a bit late when Howard reached across my desk, picked up my private line and dialed. He left a voice message, "Ali, call me when you get home. I want you to talk to a friend of mine."

I have never been the type to jump into a photograph with a celebrity or to invade their privacy in any way. In fact, I hate that sort of thing. So when I heard his message I freaked. "Howard," I declared. "You can't do that. I'm not going to make the man talk to a perfect stranger..no way...it's too embarrassing."

"Okay," he said.

Two days later, my secretary told me Howard was on the line. When I picked up I heard a familiar voice, but it wasn't Howard's.

"So, do you think I'm pretty?"

No mistaking who this was. I was going to kill Howard when I chased him down. But until then...what a complete joy. Ali and I chatted for about fifteen minutes. He told me he would have taken Mike Tyson easily because, "Tyson is slow and I could dance."

I told him about the time I took Tyson by the hand and escorted him over to meet The Chairman all the while telling Tyson that The Chairman kept boasting he could take him. "Ouch," was all Ali could manage, "Is your Chairman still alive?"

When we hung up, only a nano-second passed before I had Howard on the phone. I told him to *never do that again!* But we both knew I was very grateful to him and thrilled to have spoken with my idol.

Two weeks passed quietly. No Howard anywhere. Then, one afternoon, while I was conducting a full-staff meeting in my office, the attention of those present shifted away from my presentation. Timed like a cartoon, all the eyes in the room swept in unison toward the doorway. My gaze followed. There he stood, almost taller than the door itself.

Howard Bingham surprises Sally by bringing his friend
Muhammad Ali to her Universal office for an impromptu visit.

Well, what can I tell you? I lost it just like those kids did way back when. This time it was me clapping and cheering, throwing my arms around Muhammad Ali! What a liberating moment. Here I was, a forty-year-old movie suit losing her practiced cool. Well, damn it, some things you just have to go for, no matter how old or snooty you are.

"I came all the way here to find out something...Do you really think I'm pretty?"

There was much hilarity as I answered, "Oh yes. I really, REALLY do."

"Do you want to see me walk on air?" He began demonstrating his incredible footwork.

Movie executives are jaded by choice and experience. They're used to seeing big stars walk the hallways. If anyone appears to actually notice they instantly out themselves as newbies. The unspoken rule is that one must appear blase' at all times. But when Ali showed up everyone forgot the drill. Three floors of nonchalant employees emptied instantly into my office. What a mob scene. Everyone wanted to meet the champ including the cleaning lady. Howard Bingham slipped in quietly, and began to systematically photograph each overwhelmed fan greeting their champion. I remember watching Howard and wondering how many times in his life he had played this role?

The next week, Howard dropped by my office with a copy of each photograph personally signed by Ali. "He would be grateful," he said, "if I'd distribute each to the right person."

What started as a surprise meet and greet has turned into so much more.
Sally and Muhammad Ali share a mutual admiration for each other.

"We're the ones who should be grateful to you, Howard," I said giving him a hug. "You gave me one of the most memorable presents I have ever received...and if you do it again I will kill you."

I don't display photographs as a general rule, but I still keep the one Howard took of me with Ali in my office at home. There were many more taken over the years of the two of us and I love each one. But this particular day was special.

Later that year, I encouraged Howard to put together a book of Ali photographs taken throughout the years. I was sure it would be a best seller. I selected the shot I thought he should pitch for the cover. It is a black and white of the young, gorgeous heavyweight champion of the world taken on a visit to Kenya. At the time, Ali was considered the most famous face in the world. In this photograph, he is once again holding a small boy up in his arms. Behind him, extending as far as the eye can see, are thousands of young Kenyan children reaching up towards their hero. Howard gave me a print of this photograph which, to this day, is prominently displayed in my business office.

When times get tough, I look at this picture to remind myself what life is really all about.

Throughout my time at Universal, I had only to ask and Ali would show up for fundraising events, usually at his own expense. Once he stood for hours signing autographs long after the stars and filmmakers had ditched the scene. Howard was always in the background snapping away.

In 1996, along with millions of world-wide viewers, I watched Ali light the torch officially opening the Atlanta Summer Games of the XXVI Olympiad. I stood and applauded, even though I was alone in my living room. Not only was I thrilled for my champion, but I felt great pride and affection for my friend Howard Bingham. He was standing quietly on Ali's left, capturing the moment for posterity.

*Muhammad Ali attends the Washington DC Presidential
World Premiere of Jurassic Park to benefit The Children's Defense Fund —
an event coordinated by Sally Van Slyke.*

*Ali has spent a good deal of time and personal resources helping
out a large number of worthy causes.*

Chapter Seventeen

MR. SMITH GOES TO VEGAS

Every March the largest and most important gathering of movie theater operators in the world takes place at Bally's Resort and Casino in Las Vegas.

ShoWest is where manufacturers of new or updated movie theater products, services and technologies showcase their wares to all the major theatre circuit representatives. Mom and Pop independents and international film distributors alike attend the *ShoWest Convention* en masse. So it stands to reason that studios would use this opportunity to start buzzing, spinning—or when all else fails—fabricating ludicrous falsehoods about their upcoming roster of films.

Studios unveil their lineup with posters (called one-sheets) and trailers of coming attractions. In the rare instance a film is considered good, the attendees might get to see the entire picture.

On a side note, this show is still running. In 2010, the attendees viewed a sneak peek of major films with their fannies parked in space age, contoured seats programmed to vibrate to the music's ebbs and flows They munched on popcorn served in unbleached, grease-resistant bags and rested their aching tootsies on a prototype carpet made from reclaimed, plastic soda and water bottles. Pay green. Get green.

From the beginning, *ShoWest* attempted to treat all the studios equally. But over time, like everything else in Hollywood, them that pays the biggest bucks for the biggest bang is awarded the best spoils. At *ShoWest,* money gets you invites to the biggest, best, and most glittering galas of the convention. Although the studios put on lavish shows, the group of attendees is not very stylish. Most mom and pop independent theatre owners, hailing from Middle America, generally arrive wearing sweats. They look forward to a plethora of free movie T-shirts.

A ShoWest gala is a sit-down dinner paid for out of the studio's marketing budget. These thrilling evenings morph quickly into a monumental pain in the ass for the studio's marketing division, which now finds itself in the precarious position of having to beg overly protective celebrity publicists to enlist their unwilling clients to attend. They order in private jets for each celeb and arrange for private suites to house an entourage of bodyguards, stylists, hair and makeup experts, private assistants and significant others. This contingent is corralled, separating the notable stars from their ego boosting cortege. Once isolated, the talent is placed on an elevated dais in front of thousands of photographer hounds. Here they perch and smile for the length of the evening. Rumor was that when Barbra Streisand arrived one year with her fling Don Johnson, her entourage required three full suites. They ran up huge room service bills and hit the casino tables all courtesy of Warner Brothers.

It helps if these recognizable faces appear in films featured in the current year's *ShoWest* honor reel. This reel highlights pictures that grossed over $100M. Even if the celebrity does not have that accolade the studio finds a way to pump up their star status. If celebrity X has appeared in a recent release, they are awarded such distinctive honors as "Breakthrough Star of the Year" or "Female Star of Tomorrow." I think Paris Hilton received the latter one. In other words, just show up and an award will be found for you. After all, no votes are involved, just availability.

In 1990, *ShoWest* honored Universal Pictures by inviting us to celebrate our seventy-fifth birthday. The invitation their marketing department sent out described our gala as "a star-studded formal dinner evening." Universal had been making films for three quarters of a century. How long had I been there? It felt like I'd marketed all of them.

We appreciated the hype, but star-studded proved to be the biggest challenge. Unlike the chairmen of other competing studios, our Chairman didn't have a close coterie of talent with whom he had forged friendships. Getting a dais full of A-listers would not be easy. He did not have an abundance of favors to call in.

For instance, Steven Spielberg's Amblin Productions was built on Universal's Backlot with the studio's dime, but Steven wouldn't attend. Michael J. Fox starred in Universal's blockbuster *Back To The Future* series, but he also declined.

We were forced to try our luck with a retrospective, nostalgic approach. The only big Universal star still around from the past was Jimmy Stewart. I approached his agent and was relieved that Jimmy said yes to showing up.

Yep! Mr. Smith goes to Vegas.

We had our one big star and I hoped it was enough. However, I was worried because the night before our gala evening was the "majestic dinner." That gala dinner featured Johnny Depp, Winona Ryder, Jeff Bridges, and Tim Burton to name just a few. By comparison, we were poised to be a disappointment.

Jimmy would sit in the place of honor on the dais and at the appropriate moment would cut the five-tier cake. Not a real cake though. It was easily spotted as an ugly Styrofoam phony even from the furthest table. He would accomplish this using a flimsy wood prop-sword that looked like a sandbox reject. To goose up our lack of studdly stars, my vice president of special projects came up with an idea: When Jimmy cut the cake, a fabulous laser light show would ignite throughout the room.

Laser shows, at least at the time, were quite expensive to mount. Essentially computer controlled, they had to be carefully timed in advance to work. It was very cutting-edge electronics for the time.

The evening finally arrived. Our agenda included a VIP cocktail reception from six to seven staged in Bally's grandest VIP suite. Only the heavy hitters attending the convention, studio execs, and guest celebrities would be present. At 7 pm we all were escorted down to the ballroom by security guards. Thirty from this group were seated on a dais, crammed shoulder to shoulder. It is considered an honor to be seated on a dais. One of the folding chairs displayed my name as well, "Reserved for Sally Van Slyke."

"Please" I said humbly. "There are so many more deserving people for this honor." Who was I kidding? At this majestic gala I ranked right up there.

Pathetic.

Sadly, as Jimmy Stewart grew older he developed a weak heart. Excitement was not good for him. We asked to have oxygen standing at the ready and took the extra precaution of hiring a nurse for the evening, in case he needed medical attention.

When Jimmy and his gorgeous wife Gloria arrived, I went over the schedule for the evening carefully explaining that the ballroom would erupt with shooting lights as he cut the cake. I wanted to make sure the bright display would not startle him.

It wasn't easy to talk with Jimmy. Oh yes, he was wonderful and so very nice, but he couldn't hear a damn thing. He learned to read lips a bit, but couldn't make out zip when there was ambient background noise. Of course, Las Vegas is nothing but.

As expected, our dais was seated with non-luminaries save one. I was seated on Jimmy's right and The Chairman's left. The head of *ShoWest* was seated on The Chairman's right. So there we were, all staring at three thousand uninterested people who, ignoring our ceremonious entrance, appeared busy opening Universal's gift for this historic occasion. It was a sterling silver wine coaster designed by the legendary *Gump's* of San Francisco and engraved with the new Universal logo. I insisted on upscale and elegant. No T-shirts from us. No siree!

The Chairman knew if he turned my way he'd have to make small talk with Jimmy. So he never turned my way. It fell to me to pantomime an amusing conversation with Jimmy, because I didn't want the audience to know that our illustrious guest was deaf. Pride is important. Our conversation went something like this:

"So Jimmy, what was your favorite role?" I asked sincerely.

Assuming an answer I continued, "No kidding? Not Mr. Smith?"

Waiting the appropriate length of time I added, "Really? Oh, that is such a funny story."

Giggle. Giggle.

His mouth moved for a moment and then stopped, so I continued, "You are so right. I couldn't agree with you more...I wouldn't have slept with her either."

I was getting into the swing of it now. Those in attendance assumed a very energetic conversation was taking place between our honored mega-star and the woman next to him who looked familiar. In reality, Jimmy was just smiling sweetly and chewing.

Riveting as this fascinating dialog was, I did notice that the lights in the ballroom blinked off for about a second. It briefly crossed my mind that this was odd, but everything seemed to be on course. No one else seemed to notice.

With the rubber chicken cleared, it was finally time for Jimmy and The Chairman to step to the podium, sing Happy Birthday, cut the plywood cake, and get the hell out of there.

"Don't forget," I shouted at the top of my lungs into Jimmy's best ear. "Don't be startled by the laser lights." Just in case, I checked to make sure the oxygen was close at hand.

Clutching their sword like casting-call King Arthur's, our riveted duet missed the pre-cut insertion hole three times. Our sword was no Excalibur, but our cake was as hard as a rock. Finally the blunt thing went in. Cue the light show.

Cue the light show!!!!

Where is the light show????

Jimmy began to rock back on his heels, totally confused. He would later confess to me that he thought his eyes had selected this moment to fail on him. He thought, "Geez, if these are the golden years, you can have them."

Meanwhile The Chairman was taking it rather poorly. He was SCREAMING at me, "Do something!"

I immediately did as instructed. I looked over at my vice president of special projects who was ducking under the table. No help there. A ballroom of bored guests began packing up and pushing their way out. I catapulted off the dais, stumbled in the dark and burst into the technical area where the laser magic makers were hovering.

"What the hell happened?"

One of nature's little cataclysms that's what! Las Vegas had experienced a rolling blackout just after 8:00 P.M. which lasted for less than two seconds. Kind of like when you blow a fuse in your house. Click one

143

switch and the power is back on, but your electric alarm clock continues to blink twelve-twelve-twelve until you reset it.

There wasn't enough time to reset the complex laser program, and they had no back up in place. Not very professional boys!

Just my luck, as I was making a clean getaway with Jimmy, we bumped right into *The Hollywood Reporter's* ace snarky reporter, Claudia. She blocked our exit demanding to know who was supposed to jump out of the cake.

"It was Michael J. Fox, wasn't it," she declared.

"Yeah," I confessed. "But off the record, they stabbed him by mistake."

"Oh my God! Is he okay?" She actually bought it.

"I'm not sure. You should follow up with whatever hospital they took him to," I quipped. And with that, I spun on my heels and walked off.

We were escorted upstairs to the Universal hospitality suite to wait for the studio's executives to leave the casino tables before they signed any more markers. We planned to head en masse to a private airport (which closed at midnight) and board our plane for home. If The Chairman didn't hurry up, we'd be stuck in Sin City for the night. As I was waiting for the elevator, I found myself with a group of conventioneers who attended our gala. Usually I like to be a fly on the wall to get real feedback after an event. However, this time I would have gladly passed.

"That sucked." A rather large older woman was whining loudly and didn't care who heard her. "I mean Jimmy Stewart isn't a movie star anymore."

How soon people forget! How fickle. I just bet the old bitch watches *It's A Wonderful Life* every year and cries her eyes out.

Not yet finished with her critique, she continued, "And what the hell is this silver disc thing?"

Someone else in the group answered, "I think it's a sterling silver wine coaster."

"Hurumph!" She snarled, "Well, how cheap can they get? I mean where are the other three? What would have been wrong with a T-shirt?"

"Listen up Brahma Bull," I thought and imagined smacking her upside the head with a XXX reject from the National Dollar Store.

In contrast, the journey home was one of the most delightful experiences of my life. Jimmy entertained us with exploits he had while piloting. He continued to pilot his tiny plane well into old age—to his wife's chagrin. Gloria Stewart refused to fly with Jimmy at the controls, and wouldn't allow their twin daughters to set foot on papa's plane either.

The Stewart family lived in a traditional white colonial house on Roxbury Drive in Beverly Hills for decades. They also owned a smaller weekend home near Santa Barbara. When heading north for a getaway, overly cautious driver Gloria would pack the animals and kids into the woody station wagon. Mad bomber Jimmy would take off simultaneously and amuse himself by shadowing the car up Highway 101.

Years earlier, Jimmy was winging alone across the Midwest, stopping here and there for press interviews to tout his latest picture. Over Iowa, he suddenly encountered a brewing thunder storm and decided the smart thing to do was to set his plane down. Thankfully below him was a recently harvested field of corn. He managed to land safely. As he climbed out of the cockpit, he spied an old farmer ambling towards him. The farmer stood a short distance off gazing at this interloper for almost five minutes before he asked, "Say aren't you that feller in the moving pictures?"

"Ah...yes sir," Jimmy mumbled as only Jimmy Stewart could.

"Not smart to fly in this weather. Storm a coming." The farmer pointed up at the darkening sky.

"Yes sir," Jimmy replied. "I sure saw those coming."

The farmer looked him up one side and down the other, "You'll need a place to stay the night. No hotels in town. No good food neither. Now if you mind your manners I expect you can join the family for supper and bunk down in the barn for the night if you want."

Jimmy accepted his courtesy.

As they walked towards the main house, the farmer added, "Course there ain't much to do around these parts. But tonight's poker night and you're welcome to join us if you want."

So somewhere in Iowa on a stormy night the legendary Jimmy Stewart played poker with, "The biggest bunch of sharks I ever came across. Didn't even manage to win one hand!"

I bet it would have been fun to be a fly on that farmhouse wall!

Chapter Eighteen

FIELD OF DREAMS

The movie Field of Dreams never had anything to do with baseball, Iowa or a cornfield. Absolutely nothing.

Field Of Dreams tells the story of an Iowa farmer who walked out into his cornfield one day and heard a voice tell him, "If you build it they will come." In response, he takes down part of his cornfield, plants grass, and builds a baseball diamond.

Adapted for the screen by director Phil Alden Robinson, the story is based on the W. P. Kinsella novel entitled, *Shoeless Joe.* For those who don't know, Shoeless Joe Jackson was a pro baseball player involved in the Black Sox World Series scandal of 1919. In 1920, Jackson was banned from baseball.

Kevin Costner played Ray Kinsella, an Iowa farmer with a wife and young daughter. Plagued by financial difficulties that could force him to sell the family farm, he puts his tangible problems on hold while he follows a mysterious voice to Boston in search of 1960's author and activist Terence Mann, portrayed by the eloquent James Earl Jones. Together, the pair head to a game at Fenway Park and so the movie goes...

Universal's movie poster read, "All his life, Ray Kinsella was searching for his dreams. Then one day, his dreams came looking for him." Below these words stood Kevin Costner surrounded by clouds, hands on hips and legs crossed. Reminiscent of a scene straight out of *Bull Durham,* he looked perfectly gorgeous. This tie-in of course was intentional. At the very bottom of the poster was a small, diamond-shaped field and some hint of corn stalks.

Those in the movie business know how indispensable research is. The trick is to know when to conduct it. Unfortunately, The Chairman got the research drill ass-backwards. He'd already green-lighted this picture before he ordered up the research which indicated that women loved Kevin Costner but hated movies about baseball. I pointed out to him that *Bull Durham* seemed to do okay with the female demographic. But what did I know?

Responding to the disappointing numbers, our Chairman immediately sent down an edict: "This picture was to have absolutely nothing to do with baseball, Iowa or corn."

Interesting! The fact was we had a picture about baseball players that wasn't about baseball, which takes place with imaginary characters coming out of an Iowa cornfield, but wasn't about Iowa or corn. So what was it about exactly? Kevin Costner looking hot? Okay, I could sell that. But I thought some critics might be skeptical.

But go figure. Surprise, surprise. Preview audiences loved this movie. Grown men dissolved into tears and remained seated long after the credits rolled. In fact, there were only two people I know of who admitted they disliked this film intensely—Tina Brown the Editor of *Vanity Fair* magazine and me.

Okay, I confess. I just didn't get what all the hoopla was about. Here was this good-looking, mellow family guy who was an angry, mean adolescent jerk to his baseball-playing father. Then when daddy dies, he's overcome with remorse. Voices coming out of corn stalks give him a chance to repent by playing one more game of catch with dear old dad. I wondered why he couldn't just have been nice to dad in the first place.

Okay, you fans of Kevin. Don't hit me with a bat or start throwing spitballs at me. I admit it. I was way off base on this one.

I won't attempt to make excuses for myself. But thinking back on it, my opinion of this film was clouded during the actual filming process. It was then that I learned to despise Iowa, even though I had never been there. I promised myself to never eat another ear of corn again as long as I lived.

One day while the picture was still shooting, I received a call from an Under Secretary of the Department of Agriculture, who was checking out a formal filed complaint his office had received stating that Universal Pictures was bringing in crop planes filled with water in order to irrigate the cornfield on their movie set. If Iowa hadn't been experiencing one of the worst droughts in history, perhaps this would have gone unnoticed. Instead, it was downright offensive to the local farmers. Rain had been benched all year. The farmers, dealing bravely with a shortage of water, were about to lose their main source of revenue while some damn motion picture studio was flying in water—under cover of night no less—to grow corn that would never even be harvested.

I could see the headlines now: "Iowa Farmers, the Salt of the Earth, Picketing and Boycotting a Movie about Baseball and Farming." I wasn't sure whether to laugh or cry at the thought. This was a political nightmare that could potentially mushroom and had to be taken very seriously. I looked into the truth of the allegation and to my dismay found out it *was* true. Indeed, black helicopters were flying in at night and in stealth mode to boot. Director Robinson knew this was in the least a very insensitive move on his part. Even so, he needed healthy tall stalks for his field from which the players would emerge. What the director wants the director gets.

Short of performing an ancient Indian rain dance, there wasn't much I could do at this point. I alerted the president of production, a guy named Casey Silver, to let him know he needed to appease the locals and quickly. Fortunately for Casey, money is the universal language, and although I don't know the details, a remuneration or a donation exchanged hands quickly and the filming went on.

It turned out The Chairman was right. *Field Of Dreams* was not about baseball or even Kevin looking good. Jordan Bonfonte, senior writer for *Time Magazine* set me straight. *Field Of Dreams,* he announced, was a metaphor for father-son relationships throughout the ages. It represented every grown man's secret fantasy of connecting with dear old dad one more nostalgic time.

Oh, of course. Right. How could I have missed that? Perhaps it was the fact that I'm not anyone's son? Or was it Kevin Costner's monotone charm that lulled me into a sort of mindless half-sleep? I admit, I enjoy a good explosion every now and again, and part of me kept waiting for the old exploding baseball trick. On that long cross-country drive, did you notice he never turned the steering wheel of the VW bus? Give me something; swerving to avoid an errant cow....anything would have been nice.

This was definitely a feel good, guy movie. There aren't many of those made, and when one works, it REALLY works! Jordan figured this out when he took his young son to see a matinee of the picture, and they wept together. Jordan was so moved by his experience and those of the other fathers and sons in the theater, that he immediately placed a call to *Time Magazine's* managing editor, Walter Isaccson in New York, suggesting that they rip whatever cover was slated for next week and put Kevin Costner on instead. Walter, touched by the movie, as well as Jordan's unbridled passion, agreed.

The cover of *Time Magazine* is a BIG coup! For a movie to garner a cover instead of a war or political theme is a miracle. Celebrities are rarely considered unless they've died and most aren't prepared to go to that extreme.

Kevin was the only big star I ever worked with who did not have a personal publicist. It was terrific. I enjoyed the chance to interact with Kevin personally and really get to know him. So after hearing from Jordan, I called him directly at home. I was told he'd taken the family on vacation and could not be reached for two weeks. Oh-oh! Not the right answer. If this cover was going to happen it needed to happen right now.

I placed an emergency call to Mike Ovitz, Kevin's agent, to step in, find Kevin and make it happen. Mike was no slouch when it came to knowing what was good for business. He immediately understood how important this cover was not only for his star client but for his own growing percentage as well. Within minutes, he tracked down Kevin who was close by in Santa Barbara, hunkered down in a rented house with his kids.

Kevin didn't like being thrown a curve. He instantly balked. The answer was NO. He refused to interrupt his vacation. This didn't sit well with Mike, who flat out told Kevin not to be an idiot. I'm sure stronger words followed. Not surprisingly Kevin agreed to do the photo shoot and short interview, but only if Jordan and the photographer came to him in Santa Barbara. He would grudgingly give *Time Magazine* an hour.

If I'd heard this coming out of anyone else I would have thought he was a jerk. But I had really gotten to know Kevin and understood how much he wanted to spend time with his kids. Kevin is a good father and a sincerely nice guy. Whenever we ran into each other, I always got a warm hug which I admit was enjoyable.

These sorts of "quick" commitments often last all day. Making the kids wait, yet again, while daddy went off to do something important, could result in Kevin creating a field of dreams scenario of his own.

Of course, the one hour was stretched into a double. But the interview and photo were stellar. *Time Magazine* hit the newsstands the following Monday morning with a fabulous head shot of Kevin and cover copy that read:

Kevin Costner: "The New American Hero—Smart, Sexy and on a Roll."

Every other publication that followed called him the new Gary Cooper. Kevin hit a grand slam.

"If you build it they will come." Well, they almost came. In spite of all the publicity, *Field of Dreams* only did a decent $84M domestically.

I found it interesting that since they built a real baseball diamond and left it there on location, many did indeed come. For the next few years, tourists visited Iowa in droves, driving slowly past the lighted baseball diamond in an attempt, I imagine, to experience their own *Field of Dreams.*

Chapter Nineteen

BURGER KING RALPH

I have seen my fair share of leading men. Cary Grant enthralled me.
I got lost in the eyes of Paul Newman. Richard Harris was my fantasy.
Tom Hanks tickled more than my funny bone. And John Goodman
was about to give me—indigestion!

John Goodman, talented co-star of the television series *Roseanne*, never turned in a bad performance in front of the camera. But when it came to playing *King Ralph*, I doubt any actor, no matter how skilled at his craft, could have pulled off this 1991 Universal release. Because of this film, John Goodman abdicated his place in the Hollywood royal lineage of leading men.

A lousy script to begin with, the film was poorly directed by David S. Ward, who later went on to bring you such woofers as *Major League*. This picture was made because it was executive produced by Sydney Pollack, a man Universal wanted to keep happy.

Here's the scenario: While sitting for a family photograph, the entire British royal family is electrocuted when an exposed cable accidentally hits a puddle of water. A horrified British Government immediately jumps into action and searches for any surviving long-lost heirs. They find one distant cousin, Ralph Jones played by Goodman, who turns out to be a Las Vegas lounge singer. They fly him to England and transform him into the new King. Peter O'Toole is cast as his delightfully understanding private secretary. Sound funny to you? Well, as a studio suit, my reaction was, "Who cares?"

King Ralph was touted as "a comedy of majestic proportions" fun for the whole family. This meant it was a perfect promotional vehicle for a tie-in with a fast food chain like Burger King, for example. My promotions department could not have been more ecstatic. Fast food is the crème de la crème of movie promotion tie-ins. These drive-thru gourmet houses depend on commercial saturation for business. So you can count on them to spend major advertising bucks internationally every year.

Needless to say, Burger King jumped on board in a hurry. *King Ralph* gave Burger King a huge advertising opportunity in point-of-purchase displays, print and electronic advertising, and point of purchase giveaways. For the entire next year their advertising representatives, my promotional staff, and everyone's lawyers spent an enormous amount of time and effort maneuvering the rights, clearances, and licensing agreements required for such a massive undertaking.

The Burger King Ralph campaign would kick off one month before the actual film's release. This was fantastic. Just think of all the major advertising dollars Universal wouldn't have to spend to get the word out about this film. It was mind-boggling. My guys, and that meant me, were going to be knighted. I could hear it now: Dame Sally. Has a certain ring to it, doesn't it?

Of course, I needed the perfect photo of King Ralph—one depicting John on his throne. Who better to take this photograph than the person who, for the past several decades, had captured the royal family for posterity? His name is Anthony Armstrong-Jones, the 1st Earl of Snowdon, who also happens to be the ex-brother-in-law of Her Majesty, the Queen. Educated at the exclusive public English boarding school, Eton, Armstrong-Jones studied architecture at Cambridge and became a rather avant garde photographer about London. He married Princess Margaret in May of 1960. Now divorced from the Princess, he nevertheless remained close friends with the Windsor family.

I doubted Lord Snowdon would want to be involved with a project that essentially made fun of the royal family but I didn't see any downside to approaching him about it. I gave his agent, Peter Lyster-Todd (I just love all the hyphenated English names) a call. Peter listened politely and then cautioned, "Before I take this to Lord Snowdon, I need confirmation that you understand such a photography session will cost fifty-thousand pounds (that's about $75,000) payable in advance."

What the hell, I thought. Let's go for it. Think of all the bucks we're saving with Burger King Ralph.

Although money is money, I was amazed that Lord Snowdon

accepted the assignment and agreed to make himself immediately avail-able. Principal photography was just wrapping up at Pinewood Studios outside of London, so there was no time to waste. I flew in to oversee the photography session scheduled for John's last day of shooting. Timing was very tight. A tired, grumpy John Goodman made it clear that when the director called, "It's a wrap," he was heading for the airport and home. His bags were already packed and waiting.

Lord Snowdon arrived early the day of the shoot with his assistant and Peter Lyster-Todd in tow. He unfortunately had suffered a tumble on his way in and seemed a bit rattled when he arrived. But soon he took stock of the situation and began to set up in a small corner of the sound stage where we'd recreate a throne. I introduced myself to Lord Snowdon, who immediately instructed me to call him Tony. Over the course of the next few hours I found him adorable and charming. More importantly, he possessed a highly-trained eye, keenly aware of every detail.

Steps away from our makeshift throne, the director was shooting a formal dining room scene. This was fortunate for us because John was dressed appropriately in his kingly red with epaulets, sashes and sword. Every time the director yelled "cut" my job was to grab John and sit him on the throne. Tony, set and ready, snapped away, quietly mumbling to his assistant about any adjustments he needed to the lighting.

I was surprised that initially John seemed rather stiff, apparently awestruck with Tony. Although John was playing a king, Tony was a part of the real royalty. Peter O'Toole, the old master, detected this as well. He wandered over to loosen John up a bit. We went back and forth like this all day.

In the afternoon a key stunt-shot was filmed. In this scene King Ralph, seated at the head of a gigantic dinner table, proposes a toast to his dinner guests. He accidentally knocks over the wine glass on his left, which then tumbles into the next one, creating a domino effect down the entire row of thirty guests. Tony possessed a curious mind and wanted to understand the mechanics of the stunt. So he climbed up a ladder next to the camera-man and remained fixated on the endless takes it required to finally make it work correctly. When this was in the can, the director signaled a wrap. John changed into sweats in seconds and headed for the door. Our shoot was officially wrapped as well.

Tony was in no hurry to leave, so we sat together on the now empty set and enjoyed a bottle or two of a lovely Cabernet. Tony proved to be enormously interesting to talk to. Trained as an architect, his eye for detail kept him fascinated with life. He spoke fondly of his eldest son who'd become quite a well-known furniture designer and of his love of various published books about art—his own and others. There was no pretension to this man whatsoever. I overheard a conversation he had earlier with Peter O'Toole when I thought the aging actor overstepped his bounds. Peter, referring to the royal family, piously said, "You must feel well out of that whole mess dear boy." Tony simply smiled and walked away.

I don't remember how our conversation that evening led us to discover that we both had polio as children. I think it was because I was telling Tony how much I loved riding horses in Ireland. Tony explained how dreadful it was to be a member of the royal family and not be able to ride a horse. But he really couldn't balance well. The press actually criticized him for not participating in the sport of polo.

"Are your legs the same length?" he asked me.

"Yes," I answered. "But see, I have two different size feet." I took off my shoes to demonstrate.

"Very interesting," he said. "Now feel my legs. They aren't the same around at all."

So there I was feeling up Lord Snowdon. Then he asked if he could feel mine.

"Of course, go right ahead." I stood up to make it easy for him.

After a thorough inspection he remarked, "Well, yours are the same around. I wonder why?"

"Because," I explained, "I was lucky. I was the first kid rehabilitated under the Sister Kenny Method that essentially nixed the idea of braces. It was the tightening of the brace that retarded the growth of your leg."

"I often fall as I did this morning for no reason," he mumbled. "My leg just gives out."

"Oh, that happens to me sometimes, too," I assured him.

"How unusual."

*A note from
the Earl of Snowden,
"Dear Sally, This one dropped
off John's uniform. -
I so enjoyed meeting you
and working with
you all yesterday."
Best wishes, Tony.
Hope you enjoy Wimbledon."*

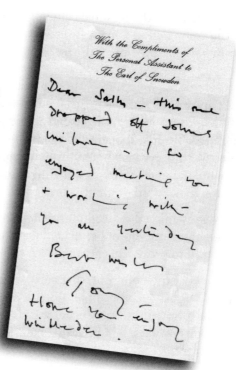

Well, we both would soon learn that it wasn't so unusual. It was the onset of post polio syndrome. Forty years after having infantile paralysis (polio) many victims experience a weakness in their legs from many years of their strong muscles having to take on extra duty.

The next day I received a hand-delivered package from Lord Snowdon which contained a sweet note thanking me for a lovely day, along with two of his books that he had autographed "to my friend with love." What a luv!

Meanwhile, back at the Universal Palace, the vice president of advertising was busy creating the *King Ralph* trailer. Not only would this footage run in the movie theaters, but it would also be edited into the Burger King Ralph commercials and promotional spots. The trailer was hilarious. The king bowling in the palace, doing his Jerry Lee Lewis act.... pure John Goodman schtick at its best. The Burger King ad executives loved it. They felt confident the promotion would be a huge success for their franchises. The national campaign pulled out all the stops and rolled out the campaign in a big way. Unfortunately, the Burger King campaign blitz helped kill the film at the box office.

Yeppers! You heard me.

On its weekend release, the movie was ranked third at the box office and nose-dived from there. Why? Because the movie stunk, that's why. The Burger King Ralph ads and the trailer had shown the only two funny scenes in an otherwise ninety-minute snore. Unhappy audiences rushed out of the theaters in droves signaling thumbs way down. The critics were even tougher. Word of mouth spread like wildfire.

Meanwhile, the production department and The Chairman all pointed their middle finger at us. We'd allowed the Burger King Ralph promotion to break too early.

Now let me point out, that early with a good movie is the preferred method. These promotional tie ins are locked, usually long before principal photography even begins on a picture, due to the fact that promotions on such a huge scale take a long time to navigate through all the channels.

Demoralized isn't even close to what we all felt about this disaster. Let's face it. Even the best, most well thought out, big-budget promotion can't electrify the audience when the movie is royally lousy.

To add insult to injury, not one major publication would consider running the Snowdon photographs because word of mouth was already so dreadful. The whole damn thing was a dismal failure unless you count my fabulous day spent with a compelling man.

Although John Goodman is definitely a big man, he is extremely light on his feet, and genuinely lighthearted and funny as well. I really thought the movie would work with him at the helm. But on set John had seemed tremendously out-of-sorts. On the last day of a shoot, actors are usually happy and excited to finish filming. Not the case with John; something felt a bit off. I suspect John Goodman's rush to leave the set had less to do with being tired and more to do with a desire to flee the scene of a super-sized bomb.

One thing John isn't is stupid.

Chapter Twenty

MY TRAMP SHINING

Some events that take place in this world are simply predestined by fate. My chance meeting with actor Richard Harris, the lovely Irish rogue with the lilting voice, clearly falls into this category

In the early seventies, I was besotted with English Repertory Theatre. The Rep offered amazing young talent fantastic opportunities to hone their craft. For instance, one brilliant Royal Shakespeare Company production of *As You Like It*, directed by the great Trevor Nunn, featured an ensemble cast that included a young Helen Mirren, Patrick Stewart, and Ben Kingsley.

In those carefree years I flew any carrier that would get me to London. Laker Airways, the favorite low-fare shuttle of the time, was my usual ride. Laker sold roundtrips from LAX to London via Gatwick Airport for $250. International students by the thousands climbed on planes wearing sweats and lugging backpacks. There was one catch to this no-frills deal. The fine print on the back of your ticket stated that a return flight was not guaranteed until you booked it from the London end.

Once, while trying to get home, I waited too long to book and was forced to wait-list on standby with TWA out of Heathrow Airport. Hours and hours went by. I had to eat the English version of cheap fast food, while working on my "really need a shower hangdog look." I finally managed to secure an empty seat. I was the last to board, except for a VIP who walked on just behind me. He was none other than King Arthur of Camelot himself, Richard Harris.

While he wined and dined in first class, I was crammed into the back row of the air-bus. No way to see more of this gorgeous creature until we arrived in customs at LAX. Once there, I stared openly as he waited in the foreign passports line. Once our passports were verified and stamped, I maneuvered my way close to him as we joined the other passengers clustered around the carousel to collect our luggage. Naturally, his bags tumbled out of the shoot first because they were tagged first-class. I watched as the immigration officials took his declaration form, looked it thoroughly over and requested that he open each of his three suitcases. These very serious uniformed officials took their time looking for contraband. In the meantime, I collected my luggage and headed out just as they completed their search. Richard Harris dutifully stood to one side during the whole inspection looking bored. Finally, and just alongside me, he was allowed through the sliding doors separating the custom area from US freedom. There in front of us was a man with a sign that read, "Harris."

I remember thinking how great it must be, *to be important enough* to have a man with a sign greet you at an airport. Then I stood and watched along with a dozen other travelers who recognized the actor, as he was escorted to the awaiting limousine. Then the tinted windows rolled-up, hiding my King Arthur from sight. My first chance encounter came to an end, but not before this gorgeous, tall, rugged, disheveled, wrinkled, twinkly, and thoroughly masculine man captured a special place in my young heart. He'd been so close to me, yet so unreachable.

Fade to black.

Flash forward to May, 1992. After fifteen years in Hollywood, I was fed up with everything and everyone. I was on the verge of selling my soul to the highest bidder. So it was time for another rejuvenating horseback ride along the Emerald Isles' Connemara Trail heading south around the Ring of Kerry. The majestic scenery, lovely people, and invigorating activity would give me the spiritual lift I needed.

To this day I love Ireland. I always rode my *special* horse, Boxer, a huge mahogany Connemara Pony, bred especially with big hooves for trekking over bogs. From the day I met him I was sure Boxer was an old lover from a past life. We understood each other. I would be so glad to see him.

I trekked with a small group of internationally diverse people. Our leader was an Irishman, Willie Leahey, who is considered the quintessential Irish master of horse breeding. I'm sure horses aren't the only thing

Willie breeds as he is also a grand master of the Irish blarney as well.

Looking over the schedule, I was pleased to note that it synced perfectly with my inner body clock. Each day we headed out after breakfast around eleven and stopped for a picnic lunch about three o'clock. I had been on this trek before, and looked forward to a picnic in a field of clover. Our rides usually included a dismount at six for a tea break and then we cantered along until eight-thirty or nine. At twilight we would stop at a convenient field and release our ponies to run free and graze with contentment. At the end of the day a van would deliver us to a lovely country hotel where we relaxed, dining heartily on simple delicious Irish country fare. We drank liberally and generally harassed the innkeeper late into the night.

Tradition was that our group of riders always gathered at a centrally located hotel in Galway the night before the trek began. The closest major airport to Galway is Shannon. Aer Lingus has a daily direct flight from LAX into Shannon. Upon landing, I met up with my hired driver who'd transport me the fifty miles or so to our hotel. More than just convenient—it was perfect. I was scheduled on an overnight flight so I could grab some undisturbed sleep. Even better, no one of Hollywood note I was acquainted with ever flew Aer Lingus. I could treat myself to absolutely innocuous solitude. Who could ask for more? No egos to pacify. No ringing phones.

In sharp contrast to my youth, these days I always flew first class. As was my habit, I requested the right window seat in Row B. No special reason except that I like it there. Once on board, I grabbed two blankets and pillows, stowed my belongings away, and zoned out in my nice, big, comfy, reclining chair with ample leg room. This was as far from the back of the bus as one could get. By the time the seat next to me was filled, I was halfway to dreamland.

BANG, SLAM, "Oh sorry, I forgot something." CLICK, BANG, sliding, ZIP, unzip, zip, BANG, SLAM. My seat began to rock sideways.

"Excuse me, do you see my seatbelt? Oh, sorry there it is."

CLICK. "Do I have time to go to the loo luv?"

The hairs on the back of my neck suddenly stood up. I peeked sideways. Destiny had arrived and was buckled in. The King was back.

I felt him look over again, "Hello," he said in his unmistakable lyrical voice.

"Hello," I replied trying not to make eye contact.

"Heading to Ireland, eh?"

"Un-huh." We were off to a sparkling start.

To my delight, he continued, "Beautiful country Ireland. You been there? I was born in Limerick, and I have family all over. Most of them have never left, ya see. Wouldn't have myself really, if I'd thought about it. You know what I mean?" He asked like he expected me to answer.

"I do. I love Ireland. I'm heading over to ride my horse along the Connemara Trail. It's mesmerizing, you know—the quiet, being able to just gaze at how beautiful it all is. I've met so many wonderful extended Irish families along the way. You are very lucky," I tried to add in a nonchalant way.

"I am, yeah," he said, putting out his hand to me and forcing me to look directly at him. "I'm Richard Harris."

"Yes," I said stupidly and then for some reason a touch too significantly I added, "I've known you for years."

God how mortifying! Of all the things I could have said: "I admire your work" or " I'm Sally" or just something that made sense but, "I've known you for years??"

With that he gave me a quizzical side-glance and went silent. I closed my eyes and wondered if he mistook me for a stalker straight out of the movie *Fatal Attraction* and suspected my next move was to boil a bunny rabbit?

It seemed hours before we were finally airborne. Once we were, the flight attendant took drink and dinner orders which, I think, made us both realize we had to speak again, or it would be uncomfortable indeed.

I began this time, "What I meant by knowing you is just that I have admired your acting and singing for many years. Your album of Jimmy Webb songs is one of my favorites, and the television movie you did of *The Snow Goose*, well, you were just so moving..." ...rattle...rattle...

This put us back on better footing, so we began to converse. I was no longer the young girl wedged in coach, but a well-traveled and enlightened woman sitting with Richard in first class. I was aglow. We talked through dinner and whispered through lights-out. All night, Richard and I exchanged confidences—sharing a magnificent sunrise. His candor made the dismal breakfast and turbulent landing bearable. My God, this man had energy.

All the while, he never consumed one drop of alcohol, which surprised me since he had a reputation as a heavy drinker. He rolled his eyes as he said, "I prefer whole milk and water now."

Richard was hilarious trying to explain rugby to me by acting out all the moves. He used a myriad of voices to verbally paint for me a picture of the haunted house he once owned with a ghost he believed resided there whom he had grown quite fond of.

As the conversation wore on, he became more philosophical and we discussed, among other things, the Catholic Church (although divorced, he still practiced Catholicism). He talked about women both in specifics and in general. This was educational to say the least. I was surprised he considered the profession of acting pathetic. (He said anyone could act.)

He recounted in fascinating detail some of his past antics with fellow actors Peter O'Toole and Richard Burton. He explained how "fucking dull" most actors actually were and described the few who weren't. It was especially enlightening when he launched into his take on how movies got made and the "horrendous sods" who made them. There was no end to what seemed to travel at top speed through his mind. This constant flow from almost anyone else would have been exhausting. With Richard, it was invigorating.

Midway through the night he asked "You married?"

"No, I'm not. I'm..."

He cut me off. "Well, good thing. I've not been a good husband..." An hour later, he had convinced me how true that probably was.

Sometime later he asked, "Do you work at something?"

"Yes, I'm a corporate marketing executive. It can be exhausting, so I need trips like this to escape the asylum. I hate all the phone calls and endless meetings. So sometimes I just leave it all behind," I said innocuously.

"Oh bloody hell," and he was off on corporations.

Clearing customs Richard asked if he could he give me a lift. He had a car waiting. We could stop in Limerick on the way. He'd introduce me to some pub mates.

"I'm a local lad made good. They'll treat you like a queen—like a movie star. You'll have fun."

I explained I had a driver waiting. My words made no difference because, once outside, Richard walked me to my car and instructed my driver that I was going to ride with him as far as Limerick and to "just follow us." I explained I was deeply flattered, but it was better I head directly to Galway for some much needed sleep.

He insisted, "Oh come on and have some fun. You'll be the center of attention!"

"I know," I laughed "and I hate that idea."

Not backing down, Richard asked, "Whatever for?"

Well, here it was...the end of the rainbow.

"Because I'm a Senior Vice President at Universal Pictures, and I've had all the star shit I can handle," I answered.

"Fuck," he said and burst out laughing. "No go?"

"Not a chance," I replied.

"Well then, I'll give you a call soon," he said, sweetly kissing me good-bye.

That sounded lovely actually, but I knew he wouldn't. He didn't even know my last name or where I'd be for the next two weeks.

Two weeks is an eternity. Out of sight, out of mind. Reality sucks.

"Bye Richard" I said. "You will remain my fantasy forever." With that I left.

The seventh day of our trek on the south coast of Ireland was particularly blustery. We rode with newspaper shoved down our leggings

Sally and her horse Boxer, on the Emerald Isles' Connemara Trail.

for warmth and covered by "dry as a bone" Australian style coats. These are long waxed tarp-like overcoats equipped with leg snaps that prevent billowing in the wind. I adored riding through the mist and rain, hoofs clamoring over the bogs as we made our way up to the very top of the highest brilliant emerald hill where our only company was the Angora sheep, coats thick, ready for shearing.

I was the only American on the trip, from sunny California no less, a fact that amused everyone. I was also the only rider to carry a flask of brandy. A stiff wallop would ward off any real chill. We paused briefly at the very top of the tall hill, gazing at the ever-changing breathtaking view of the green Irish countryside.

I was having a wee nip to fortify me for the long slippery slope down, when Willie spied a rider coming straight for us at a full gallop. His speed was dangerous enough to indicate an emergency. Perhaps a rider behind us had taken a serious fall and needed medical help, or a horse had gone badly lame for some reason.

Photograph taken of Sally by Richard Harris outside of Limerick, Ireland.

This courier of bad news was waiving a sign and signaling us. Finally reigning in just alongside our group, he reached into his pocket, pulled out a huge phone and announced, "I have a phone call for Sally Van Slyke." As he opened his mouth, my eye fell on the sign. It was a copy of the Universal Pictures logo.

It would be fun to tell you I screamed bloody murder at Richard right then and there. Alas, cell phones didn't work well on Irish hilltops.

I didn't talk to Richard until I was back in my room. After downing five or six straight shots of Irish whiskey, the phone rang. On the other end was Richard. Extremely sober and heartily amused with his clever self, he soon figured out he'd reached a very toasted Sally Van Slyke. I had a wonderful time knocking about my room while we talked into the wee hours of the morning. Frankly, Richard had a hard time getting a word in edgewise. Now that's saying something.

Richard was in London but wanted to meet me in Limerick on my way home. I was rested and relaxed when we finally hooked up. Limerick is not terribly small but it still maintains the charm of a small Irish village. Richard showed me one of the best times of my life. He was related to or knew everybody.

We walked together in the surrounding fields full of vivid, colorful wild flowers lilting in the wind. I asked Richard to hold my camera while I picked a nosegay. This was before digital cameras. Everyone shot film. It was weeks later in LA before I got around to picking up the developed pictures and realized Richard had taken some photographs of me. One is very special, in part because it captured a happy lady surrounded by clover with her hair flowing back in the wind, but mostly because he had captured the great joy I had found in the power of destiny.

If you ever get the opportunity to pick up an old copy of Richard Harris's album called *A Tramp Shining* on which the best known song is "MacArthur Park," do it. It is both musically and lyrically compelling.

Richard Harris will forever be my tramp.... shining.

Chapter Twenty-One

UNIVERSAL ORLANDO

*If the ride American Tail breaks down, at least Fievel
won't get loose and eat the tourists. Wanna bet?*

Universal Studios' first foray into the world of theme parks was in Orlando, Florida marked with a giant celebration, incredible hype, and total disaster.

Although I didn't usually get involved with theme parks (I don't even like them), I was asked to attend the Orlando opening. I was charged with the responsibility of corralling the celebrities in attendance, making sure they showed up to scheduled events on time, and, for the most part, intact.

I arrived on the scene two days before the grand opening. The humidity in Orlando was wilting my enthusiasm fast. Within eight hours of arrival, I'd already had it with the whole scene. Not only was I forced to suffer through frizzy bad-hair days, but almost everything else was on the fritz as well.

For example, the day I arrived David, the park's marketing guru, held me captive and forced me to listen as he rehearsed his opening oration. Riveting as his speech was, I interrupted his dirge to point out that the riverboat making a test voyage behind him was sinking head first into the mock Mississippi mud. Was something amiss? After all, the film *Titanic* had yet to be made.

That same afternoon, one of the park executive's wives, while waiting patiently to take a spin on the final test run of the *American Tail* 3-D thriller ride, tumbled head first into an uncovered six-foot hole in the floor. No one had noticed this makeshift dungeon because, although the ride was functioning perfectly, the safety lights had completely crapped out. The Jaws of Life were called in to get this injured hysterical woman out of the tight squeeze without breaking her *other* leg.

The day before the official public opening, Michael J. Fox and Steven Spielberg winged in to honor the new state-of-the-art thrill rides based on Universal's hit films *Back To The Future* and *Jaws*.

Later, a chartered 747 flew in a host of other recognizable faces. To be perfectly truthful, most of these, "Hey, haven't I seen you someplace before," faces weren't exactly the A-listers an adoring young theme park fan base would most want to see. The celebrities included such names as Ernest Borgnine, Angie Dickenson, and Henry Mancini. All lovely people, but not very exciting or press worthy.

Rounding out this parade of celebrities at the eleventh hour was Sylvester Stallone. He was apparently coerced into showing up by his agent Ronnie, who was attempting to negotiate a big deal with Universal at the time. (FYI: he is now the President of Universal Studios) Sly's private Lear jet had just landed when Rocky got a gander at the celebrity list. Without saying a word, he headed to the hotel and proceeded to lock himself in his rooms, refusing to come out for the evening's VIP reception. Naturally, it fell to me to coerce him out of lock-up.

I began by ringing his suite several times. He wouldn't pick up the phone. So I headed over to his side of the hotel and rang the doorbell.

Nothing.

So I resorted to violence, knocking loudly with my fists. This finally garnered a response.

"Go the hell away," Rocky snarked.

"Oh, come on Sly," I tried the old ego approach first. "You are always the biggest star at any gathering, you know that!"

"Well, okay, yeah," I knew he'd agree. "At least I recognize some of the other people on the list. Are they important? I thought Angie Dickenson was dead."

I could tell at this point he was standing just on the other side of the three-inch solid oak door with the triple bolt action lock. "Come on Sly, just open the door and let's chat reasonably about this. Steven and Michael are here."

"Yeah, sure they are cuz *they* got rides. They didn't make me a Rocky Balboa ride. So why am I here?" At least he was talking.

That was a good question, but I didn't have time to think of a bullshit answer because lookie-loos were beginning to step off the elevator and stare at me. By the looks on their faces, I think they assumed I was hollering through the door at a cheating, no-good spouse. Or worse. I was the cheating no-good spouse.

"Please, can we just talk a minute?" I pleaded.

"I'm not talkin' about anything. I'm calling Ronnie. Then I'm calling room service." With that, the conversation ended.

I walked down the hallway trying to avoid eye contact with bystanders who were eavesdropping and misreading the situation. This was just too much. I hastily left the scene and reported to all concerned that Sly was a bit under the weather. By the way, he would have been if he'd let me in. I'd have Rocky Balboa'd his stubborn ass.

That evening we learned a major thunderstorm was predicted to hit within the next eighteen hours. Who were the nitwits who said, "The show must go on," or "Tomorrow is a brand new day"? What the hell did they know?

Opening day celebrations kicked off with a bleacher crashing loudly to the ground, narrowly missing my head and several hundred paying guests happily anticipating the festivities.

As the parade rolled slowly down Main Street, the convertible carrying Ernest and Tova Borgnine stalled, completely blocking the middle of the road. This caused loud gaffaws and a disappointing lull in the proceedings until AAA showed up with a tow. I thought it might be time to pray.

At long—oh so long—last, we were all gathered up on the makeshift stage. My prayers were answered when the flying DeLorean from *Back To The Future* managed to arrive on cue, time traveling itself into place. Michael J. Fox emerged and proceeded to do his very funny movie character shtick, tripping out of the vehicle as Marty McFly. Unfortunately, the cameras all swooped in front, blocking the view for most of the paying guests.

"Boo! Boo!"

His bit completed, Michael attempted to leave the stage unnoticed. We weren't prepared to have him depart yet, and this created an instant security breakdown of massive proportions. He was immediately mobbed by fans, who jumped off the bleachers practically landing on top of his head and completely surrounding him. Michael is diminutive in size, and we quickly lost sight of him in this mass of humanity.

Frightened for him, the guards, my staff, and I flung our bodies up and over the crowd in an attempt to rescue the poor guy from being literally trampled to death. My dress was ripped to shreds, and the VP of promotions lost both his tasseled loafers and jacket along with everything in his pockets. We grabbed hold of Michael and formed a circle around him by linking arms. Shoving back the crowd, we hustled him to safety.

At about five in the afternoon the storm struck. The deluge of rain began to fall just as all the celebrities were scheduled to attend yet another VIP cocktail soiree in the theme park reception hall. Many lacked the pluck to combat the storm and never showed up. Our proud Chairman of MCA, Lew Wasserman, tried valiantly to drive to the location in a covered golf cart but couldn't manage to find the building. It was literally hidden from view by the massive downpour. I caught sight of him circling around and around with his wife riding shotgun. She was yelling up a storm of her own. Meanwhile, David, the park guru, presented his rehearsed dissertation to a near-empty room. Everyone agreed it was the best speech he ever made.

Party in the tank, so to speak, there was not one more damn thing to do. So my staff and I went off to ride the new *Jaws* adventure. I adore Brucie the shark with his toothy Crest-like grin.

We lined up right along with the paying guests. At the last minute, Spielberg and Stallone decided to put in an incognito appearance and jumped into the front seats. My staff and I sat right behind them on the trawler.

A pretty, newly trained, young tour guide took her place at the helm of the boat and began her spiel. She smiled at the front row, swallowed hard and stated in a clear, confident voice, "Welcome to Amity Harbor! Let's up the anchor and go fishing, shall we?"

Okey dokey!

The ride moved forward.

"What could be lurking up around this cove?" she whispered conspiratorially into her headset.

Suspense built rapidly. Our collective hearts were pounding now. We could hear the crash of the waves hitting the shore. This was odd because we were supposed to be in the middle of the ocean. I was sure that was a little bug they were still working out.

"Watch out on your left," she suddenly screamed!

We all simultaneously turned to our left. What were we watching out for? Nothing was out there.

"That was a close one, wasn't it?" she sighed with obvious relief.

OK, if you say so. This was obviously another *bug* that needed to be worked out. I looked behind me. Everyone was still hanging off the left side of the boat to see what they missed. Steven was searching a bit more diligently than the others, looking a bit queasy. Was he getting seasick? We continued to trawl along. Chug. Chug.

"Take cover...I see him coming alongside our right flank..." our guide shrank back in horror.

Everyone braced for action. We spun to our right. Nothing. Again nothing. We couldn't even spot a guppy. Then the grumbling began.

"Excuse me, we don't seem to be moving anymore."

"Are we stuck in the lagoon? Is the ride broken?"

"Mommy, you said we would see a shark," said an adorable little girl perched on her daddy's lap. "I have to go baffroom. I wanna go home!"

Not the adventure ride our illustrious band of Hollywood muscle had hoped for. Brucie was a no show. It was heartbreaking to watch our young tour guide's eyes swell with tears, especially in front of Steven Spielberg and Sly Stallone. These fellas can be a little short on sympathy, particularly when one of them has a cut of the gross proceeds from the adventure ride at hand. Steven's neck was craning around, no doubt looking for a fall guy.

Although I was in no way responsible for the quality of the rides, it is common practice in Hollywood to instantly assign blame. Culpability has little to do with guilt, rather proximity is all that is needed. So guess on whom Steven's piercing eyes were about to land? Let me tell ya mateys, I couldn't get off that boat quickly enough. I would gladly have dived head first into the shark-infested waters. But there wasn't much water left in this ocean, much less ferocious fish.

Bright and early the next morning, the sun was out and all was tranquil. At breakfast, everyone was talking about the mini-tsunami that struck Cabot Cove the previous evening. On our theme park map, I noticed Cabot Cove was located next door to Amity Harbor. Fortunately, no one had been injured as I'm told Jessica Fletcher *(Murder She Wrote)* had the situation well in hand and had invited everyone to dine al fresco on a delicious fresh fish catch.

Meanwhile back on Amity the hunt was still on for Brucie.

Chapter Twenty-Two

AND THE OSCAR GOES TO...

When people learn I'm a member of the Academy of
Motion Picture Arts and Sciences (AMPAS), they inevitably
whisper to me that they would dearly love to attend the
Oscars just once in their life.

No, I tell them, you actually wouldn't. Unless nominated or
presenting, most Hollywood A-listers prefer to head straight to
the Oscar after-parties, skipping the main event. That's really
where all the action is.

Every year, millions of viewers worldwide tune in to watch the Oscar telecast from the comfort of their homes. These lucky people (I am now one of them) can view the festivities in their pajamas. Or, they can watch Joan Rivers trash the stars' outfits, while they wear absolutely nothing at all. When, **not if**, things start to get boring, they can hit the refrigerator for something alcoholic and cold. They are free to make all the noise they want opening the bag of potato chips and they can jump up and go to the bathroom at will. Best of all, they can switch the channel during the really dull parts.

If I'm speaking to a man, and the subject of "loving to attend the Oscars" comes up, even die-hard movie buffs make sure I understand that he doesn't want to go, but it would make their wife, partner, or lover so very happy. In the case of attending the Oscars, the wife, partner, or lover wouldn't really be as thrilled as you might think. Let me tell you why.

First of all, the Academy Awards is a long, grueling evening which begins mid-morning when one must obsess over hair, nails, makeup, and Spanx to be ready in time. Then you spend a minimum of three hours in a limousine inching its way forward on jam-packed streets. God help you if you have to drive yourself. Mercifully, I never did.

Okay, I admit it. The first year I was excited to go.

Just a few years ago, the Kodak Theatre opened on Hollywood Boulevard. This state-of-the-art facility now houses the Awards Ceremony which is broadcast in February on a Sunday night. Before that, however, the Awards were held on a Monday night in late March or early April, and the venue alternated between the Shrine Auditorium and the Dorothy Chandler Pavillion. Both are smack in the middle of congested downtown Los Angeles.

My first foray into this glamorous celebration was a Monday in April. The temperature in LA had soared well over a hundred degrees by noon. I broke into a full sweat just getting from my front door to the limo parked five feet away. I was joined this evening by four male associates, all single, at least for this night.

We spent the next two hours talking sports statistics while inching our way along the sweltering freeway. The asphalt was so hot I swear it was bubbling. Attempting to compensate for any discomfort from the heat, our driver cranked up the air conditioning to what I believe was a cool zero degrees.

Now the guys were just fine. They wore tuxedos and each one put his jacket back on. I, on the other hand, wore a gorgeous full-length, pale green, strapless, chiffon dress with a low back. When the air conditioning hit my shoulders, the rivulets of sweat cascading down my back began freezing into stalactites. I suggested we turn the air conditioning down just a wee bit before I caught pneumonia, but I was overruled by the back-seat jocks.

The Academy states emphatically that the entrance doors will close at 4:30 pm. Guests must be in their seats by 4:55. If guests are not prompt, they will be locked out of the auditorium until the first commercial break. In this case, being locked out meant missing Billy Crystal's monologue, sure to be the best part of the evening. Billy Crystal is a riot, especially when the cameras are off.

At precisely 4:35 pm, our limo was surrounded by at least thirty more just like it still three stadium-length blocks away from the entrance to the Shrine Auditorium. If we wanted to see Billy, there was nothing to do but get out and run for it.

We leapt from the car and began to jog. The boys had the advantage of flat bottom patent leather shoes, while I had to navigate the cracked sidewalk in 4-inch heels. We raced past the other limos. Our idea must have been a good one; the once empty sidewalk became a virtual sea of penguins and sequins all clomping and clattering down the street. Glancing to my right, I saw a very pregnant Glenn Close challenging the lead at a breakaway gallop.

Let me tell you, there is nothing like slogging a four-minute mile through a steam bath to get the ol' juices flowing. At least I was thawing out, but then so was my hair which had that limp overly-sprayed look we ladies just love. It was going to be a toss-up which to fix first: the hair or the makeup running down my face and neck and into my delicate decolletage.

Panting audibly in synchronized rhythm, we all rounded the corner and sprinted down the red carpet with exactly one minute to go. There was no time for photos, a glass of water, or a bathroom fix. I made it into my seat with three seconds to spare.

"Good evening and welcome to the......." We were live to the East Coast.

Billy Crystal was on stage and in rare form. The cameras followed his every move. He brilliantly sang, danced and snarked his way through the monologue, not a drop of sweat on him. To keep the stage area at a bearable temperature for the talent, the air conditioning was cranked full blast in the auditorium. Billy was comfortable. However, I sat there laughing hysterically while gusts of frigid air morphed me into an ice sculpture.

If you leave your seat to go to the bathroom during a commercial break, you must make it back by the end of the break, or you will be locked out until the next pause for sponsors. One of a hundred black tied seat-fillers will sit in your place, so that the audience always appears full on camera.

The Shrine Auditorium, home to many rock concerts and expo events, is a building long past its prime. The inadequate bathrooms are located down a perilously steep break-neck flight of stairs off the front lobby. If you can climb Mt. Everest, you probably wouldn't have a problem, but maneuvering down in Jimmy Choo's is a challenge. I wobbled down, trying not to step on my dress to avoid arriving headfirst. Safely down the slippery slope, I cued up behind a mile of anxious women all waiting their turn. While in line, I passed the time by fixating on *Entertainment Tonight's* Mary Hart who was valiantly struggling to side step down the mountainside in a skin tight, red sequined dress and four-inch stilettos. Miraculously, she stayed on her feet. What a pro. Other ladies weren't so fortunate. "Timber" was often called as we graciously stepped out of the way.

Finally my turn arrived. Propping open the stall door, I engaged in hand-to-hand combat with my dress. I attempted bravely to sandwich my body and miles of flowing chiffon into this four by four cell without dragging my light and lovely creation through the stagnant and ever so pungent puddle of overflowing toilet water pooling under my feet. Once I was pointed in the right direction, I frantically searched for a place to park my purse. No shelf or hook to be found, I finally just clenched the damn thing between my teeth and shut the door.

Of course, no woman ever managed to make it back to her seat in one commercial break. The average was three. Getting back up the stairs was tough. Then, of course, there was the small matter of disengaging the sodden toilet paper from your shoe.

I was lucky to be back in my seat for "And that's it for the...." Mercifully, this signals the entire audience to rush out into warmer air.

Immediately following the telecast (the West Coast airing is on time delay), the Governor's Ball kicks into high gear in an adjacent hall or tent. Not every audience member is invited to the Ball. One must hold a separate ticket for this pleasure.

Each year, as part of the media hype, the dinner menu for the Ball is touted to the world via various magazine and morning shows. Super star chef, Wolfgang Puck, has catered the dinner for many years. This is no easy task and requires hundreds of service chefs and prep cooks just to plate the three-course meal. Moving it out onto the floor are several hundred servers running relay with track shoes on. Wolfgang's desserts taste as wonderful as they look. This particular year, he served a hand-crafted golden Oscar filled with chocolate mousse and fresh berries. Unbelievably tricky to make, if allowed to warm up at all it would melt.

Yes! It all sounds marvelous, but in reality it never is.

In the first place, it is a monumental task for any caterer to serve hundreds of guests a plated three-course dinner from a makeshift kitchen comprised of butane ovens, stovetops, heating racks, and dry ice for keeping product cold. I don't care how famous you are—the Governor's Ball is a mighty task magnified tenfold.

Hollywood thrives on the motto "see and be seen." As a result, absolutely no one sits in one place for long at the Ball. They're over here for a kiss-kiss and then over there for a hug-hug. Even the most experienced banquet servers become frazzled in seconds. They're serving the table when suddenly no one is sitting there.

"But they were just there a moment ago!"

By the time a server gets a plate in front of a stationary body, the food is already stone cold. (Except in the case of the gold statuette. It melted into a big plop from all the body heat.)

Guests who neglected to eat lunch so they wouldn't have any belly pooch showing on the walk down the red carpet might perch long enough to eat something. Tom Hanks and Rita Wilson sat down at our table for ten minutes to stave off starvation and then were off. Kiss-kiss!

One bite and then it was time to follow everyone to the post-Oscar bashes. The most famous of these intimate soirées for hundreds is hosted by *Vanity Fair* magazine. Very chic. Elton John, in support of his AIDS charity, jumped into the fray a few years ago and his party is a must show as well. Trying to get to either is a nightmare. Once again, limos idle in long lines as the celebrities of the moment step forward for the cameras,

"Look over here Angelina!" Flash. Flash. Flash.

All went well this particular night. Sometimes though, someone gets a bit testy and all hell breaks loose. Mickey Rourke comes to mind in the "could-get-out-of-hand" category. In these cases you have to be fast on your feet to avoid the path of destruction. But don't worry because this sort of mayhem usually happens while the average Academy reveler is still stuck at the theater trying to locate their limo.

When disembarking from the limo for the evening the party-goer is given a claim check with the limo call number on it. At the end of the evening, he or she presents this claim check to one of many limo expediters who pages your limo via walkie-talkie.

"Calling up number 94500980...over."

Responding number 92500409...over."

Sputter. Hiss. (Nowadays that would translate to, "My phone just cut out" or, "Sorry, must have texted the wrong number.")

"No bro, I said number 94500980...over."

Hiss. Crackle.

"Yo, bro, s'up with this thing." All expediters seem to be from Jersey. I think it's a law.

Once the right limo responds, there is another wait for your driver to make it to the front of the line. While waiting for what seemed like forever, I asked myself silently, "Would this happen to Julia Roberts?" The answer is "yes." Julia was standing right next to me.

We finally made it to the first party on our list.

Entertainment Tonight reported the next day, "It was a magical evening.... the drinks were flowing..." Oh yeah? Well, they hadn't been flowing in our direction unless you count getting a glass of wine spilled all over you.

How much fun can one person stand? All that really mattered was that tomorrow we could all say we had been there. Nothing like making our lesser counterparts feel jealous.

Right now, I wanted to be somewhere else and not at another party. We headed out, hit some late night, fat-burger joint that served hooch, and got sloppy drunk. Now this was starting to be fun, because it wasn't long before a few of the other festive revelers got the same idea and joined us. Thank God this was an all-night dive.

Even after this traumatic first experience, I continued to attend the Oscars every year. I didn't have much choice since I ran the Academy campaigns. From then on though, I showed up wearing a dress with sleeves and carrying a wrap. I arrived each Oscar night with my fingers crossed, hoping our campaign was a success. I'm glad to report that we were often very lucky.

So in conclusion, my dear ladies and gentlemen, if you still want to attend the *Academy Awards,* all I can say is, just be careful what you wish for. My advice is to stay home, say anything you want about the dresses, the hair, and be your own Joan Rivers. That's what I do. I can't tell you how simply wonderful it is to ignore my invitation every year.

See you at the Oscars!